OPINIONS

OF THE

INDIAN ARMY

OPINIONS
OF THE
INDIAN ARMY

STUDHOLME JOHN HODGSON

GYAN

Published by

Gyan Publishing House
5, Ansari Road
Daryaganj, New Delhi-110002
Phone: 011-47034999, 9811692060
E-mail: books@gyanbooks.com

Distribution Network
gyanbooks.com
India, USA, Canada, UK, Australia

ISBN: 978-93-7014-063-9 (PB)

First Published, 1857

2nd Impression 2025

Printed at: Gyan Press, Delhi.

OPINIONS OF THE INDIAN ARMY
Author: STUDHOLME JOHN HODGSON

OPINIONS

ON THE

INDIAN ARMY.

(ORIGINALLY PUBLISHED AT MEERUT IN 1850, UNDER THE TITLE OF "MUSINGS ON MILITARY MATTERS.")

BY

COLONEL JOHN STUDHOLME HODGSON,

BENGAL ARMY.

BRIGADIER, LATE COMMANDING THE PUNJAB IRREGULAR FORCE.

LONDON:

W. H. ALLEN & CO., 7, LEADENHALL STREET.

1857.

THE MOST NOBLE

THE MARQUIS OF DALHOUSIE, K.T.,

GOVERNOR - GENERAL OF INDIA.

MY LORD,

In availing myself of your Lordship's permission to inscribe to you these unpretending pages, I feel that I best serve the interests of that Army, with a view to whose welfare they were written.

Fully convinced as I am of the great merits of the native soldiery, I have not hesitated to point out those merits, at the same time that I have honestly stated their defects.

To your Lordship, as descended from a race of soldiers, and as the Ruler of a great empire, your administration of which has been signalised by the addition of a new kingdom to the British territories, I am confident that the well-being of a large portion of those troops, whose gallantry and devotion have been mainly instrumental in effecting that principle, must ever be a subject of the deepest interest; and if anything which a long personal intercourse with the native troops, and a close observation of them, has enabled me to suggest in the following pages, should happily prove of use in effecting the amelioration of the moral and physical condition of the Sepahee, my object in having written on this important subject will have been fully answered.

I have the honour to subscribe myself,

My Lord,

Your Lordship's most obedient

and humble Servant,

J. S. HODGSON, Brigadier,

Commanding the Punjab Irregular Force.

Lahore, December, 1850.

OPINIONS ON THE INDIAN ARMY.

Section the First.

DESULTORY REFLECTIONS AND OBSERVATIONS ON VARIOUS SUBJECTS IN CONNECTION WITH THE MORALE OF THE NATIVE ARMY OF INDIA: CALLED FORTH, BY THE PERUSAL OF A LETTER, LATELY RECEIVED FROM A VERY OLD AND MERITORIOUS NATIVE OFFICER—AN OFFICER DECORATED WITH ALL THE HONORARY INSIGNA OF THE SERVICE, AND WHO IN HIS CAREER HAD SEEN MUCH ROUGH WORK IN THE FIELD, AND IS NOW REPOSING ON HIS WELL EARNED LAURELS, AFTER A USEFUL AND HONOURABLE SERVICE OF SIXTY YEARS.*

AMONG the many interesting and graphic anecdotes related by this gallant pattern of old fidelity, one occurs to me as happily illustrative of a portion of the subject, proposed to be discussed. Says the Subadar: — "During the campaign

* The following pages, written in the casual manner usually adopted in contributing to a newspaper have gradually increased to the present size. Professional duties prevent the author from revising what he has from time to time sent to the press. But in the hope that hurriedly as they have been committed to paper some of these remarks and suggestions, the result of long experience and heartfelt interest in the native army may be useful to the service, he publishes them at once with all their imperfections rather than impair any interest they may possess by delaying till he could command leisure to amend them.

against the Mahrattas, in the year 1804, we made a tremendous forced march of fifty-four miles in thirty hours, and surprised Holkar, and his cavalry at Furruckabad, and routed them with great slaughter. We had marched 250 miles in thirteen days. The troops had been upon very short commons for some time, and you, Sir, know what a tyrant a hungry belly is. The Sepahees began to be very loud in their grumblings, and expressed their discontent pretty freely. This was reported. A short time afterwards, Lick Sahib Bahadoor (Lord Lake) was observed riding past the column *eating dry pulse.* This fact spread rapidly through the ranks, and from that moment not the whisper of a murmur was heard. I believe, Sir, had a man grumbled after that, he would have run the risk of being put to death by his comrades; such was the love and veneration the Sepahees had for Lick Sahib Bahadoor. Khodawund, Lick Sahib Bahadoor, *poora* Sepahee tha!" (Lick the Hero *was* a thorough soldier, Sir).

Though the noble Ancient often repeated this anecdote during a camradeship of twenty-four years, yet he never varied or embroidered it in the slightest particular. It might have been tact on the part of that truly great soldier, Lord

Lake, and no doubt it was; but it was the tact that never could have occurred to a little mind, which, in all likelihood, might have resorted to some harsh martinet measures to stifle this expression of human suffering, and thereby increased the discontent, if not have roused feelings still more dangerous.

Surely it must be apparent to the most superficial observer, that the present system of the native army requires some reformation to suit the altered state of things, and their daily changing aspect.

The wisdom of experience has determined, that every state should possess within itself a power of periodical reformation, with a capacity of checking, and eradicating, from time to time, all abuses, and introducing such wholesome changes as may be required to give additional vigour and vitality to the political system. These sound principles are in every respect applicable to a great standing army, but more especially to the native army of India, organised out of such peculiar and conflicting elements. The Government of India has done much to ameliorate the condition of the European soldier, and it might with an equally wise and beneficent foresight bestow some similar consideration on the Sephaee. Never was there an army so well paid, so well treated, or so generously cared for in most respects, and yet whose moral and physical improvement has been more neglected, than that of the native army of India. Little or no attention, it would seem, has hitherto been attracted to this most important subject. The Sepahee's physical and moral culture solely consists at present in being drilled, clothed, and accoutred in the British uniform. This alone does not make a soldier. A soldier must be proud of his profession, simple and hardy in his habits, inured to labour, imbued with a generous and martial spirit, and ever actuated by an unalterable and devoted feeling of loyalty to the Government he serves. There is good stuff in the Sepahee, which admits of higher cultivation, but the stimulus must be given by the ruling powers themselves.

If, unwisely, the Sepahee is invariably to be considered and treated as the mere vulgar and sordid mercenary, then nothing should be neglected which may conduce to the one all absorbing conviction forcing itself on his mind, that his worldly interests are so interwoven with the stability of British rule in India, as to have become inseparably identified with its safety and duration. Motives of self-advantage, as a national trait, appear to be the very strongest incentives to action, on the part of the Asiatic; in whose language gratitude has absolutely no place.

This is not mentioned in a cynical spirit, but simply to state a fact, and one which in some degree elucidates the peculiar character of oriental attachment.

"Jis ka Deg, oos ka Teg"*

is one of their most popular, and admired Sepahee aphorisms, and would appear to contain the very essence of their estimation of mercenary virtue.

But surely *these* are not the feelings to which a great and wise Government is to address itself, when legislating for a highly disciplined army of near 300,000 men, aliens in blood, prejudices, and religion?

Most unquestionably it ought not to be so. The Sepahees of this army have given abundant proofs that in them the highest feelings of human nature are susceptible of being worked upon with the most brilliant results. The military classes possess a high sense of honour, with a strong desire for distinction and applause. There are no men more easily excited by praise or flattery, or more capable of great exertion under such influences.

* "He who can keep the pot boiling,
Will never want for trenchant *blades*."

Under those truly illustrious commanders who so thoroughly understood and appreciated them, what distinguished services have they not rendered to the British nation!

The magnificent superstructure of glory and dominion which British enterprise has so triumphantly erected in the East, *mainly* rests on the wise, ever just, and liberal recognition of those noble and all important services.

The day we undervalue the Sepahees, or weakly betray symptoms of a want of confidence in their fidelity and loyalty, will be a fatal one for the honour and the stability of this empire.

Any one act on our part, significant of the existence of such a cruel suspicion, would most effectually and irretrievably destroy that implicit confidence which the men, at the present moment, so unreservedly repose in the justice and integrity of the British Government, and, confidence, like honour, once lost, is lost for ever!

They would necessarily be under the ever constant apprehension, knowing that such distrust existed, of experiencing some fearful and signal mark of the anger of the British Government. The army would from that day cease to be a popular service with our native subjects. And even the unfortunate wight whom the pressure of a hard necessity might force into our military employ, would exclaim: "My poverty but not my *will* consents!" Are we to reply "we pay thy poverty, and not thy *will?*"

If so, what becomes of the attachment and fidelity of the native army?

There will not be wanting some who will observe "So long as our pay is regular, so long will there be no difficulty in recruiting the ranks of the native army." Granted.

But are the feelings and motives of those taking military service with us, of no present importance, and of still less serious consideration as affects the future? This mutual confidence *once* shaken, the gold and temptations of any other power, able and willing to purchase treason, would prove too strong for the loyalty of *any* army, based on such insecure foundation. Such allegiance, if it be not a mockery to call it for an *instant* by that honest name, would palpably admit of easy and unblushing transfer.

But such a fatal error as questioning, on light grounds, the temper and fidelity of the native army, is one most assuredly not likely to be committed, so long as honour and justice are dear to Englishmen, and the characteristics of British rule.

The faithful and devoted services of a hundred years, and the inviolate good faith which has ever existed between the British Government and her noble Indian army, are the best securities for the lasting preservation of this happy and honourable state of feeling.

A calm, wise, and dispassionate legislation is all that is now required to consolidate the triumphs of genius and enterprise. There is no country under the face of the sun more likely to be dangerously convulsed than India by any erratic flights of rulers, meanly ambitious of obtaining for their individual selves a spurious and inflated pre-eminence.

On looking back upon the history of our acquisition of this mighty empire, one cannot fail to be sensibly struck with the combination of fortuitous causes which has so remarkably attended our progress to power and dominion.

It is very clear that the great secret of our success has been a most judicious and careful avoidance of every act that could justly alarm the religious and conventional prejudices of the natives of India, or call in question our national good faith. Indeed, the arts and superior handicrafts of civilization are the only safe schoolmasters and missionaries of a backward state of society.

There have not been more horrors or frightful atrocities committed in the name of Liberty, than in that of Religion. The wonderful sagacity of Columbus gained for Spain a new world, but that priest-ridden country was unequal to the task of founding a great empire. What should have been a glory, became her just punishment and humiliation. She attempted to force upon a new people a religion unknown to them and their forefathers; and, in that frantic and abortive attempt, she perpetrated unheard-of cruelties, and nearly extirpated the interesting population of the New World; instead of showering the blessings of peace and civilization around, she stained her path with blood and devastation.

Spain was unworthy of the splendid destiny that fortune had offered her. We have providentially escaped these fearful errors. And honour be to those to whom honour is due. Clive! Warren Hastings! Cornwallis! Wellesley! Hastings! What glorious images of energy and transcendent abilities these time-honoured names awaken! How truly happy was the British nation in such an extraordinary succession of able rulers, who appeared at momentous junctures, and before whose master minds and statesmanlike views, difficulties became but stepping-stones to greatness. The edifice they have raised, the wonder of the world, will yet appear still more wonderful to far more civilized generations to come.

The chief prop and bulwark of this stately structure is a disciplined native army of nearly 300,000 men; held together, *solely*, by an unlimited confidence in the just appreciation of its British rulers.

What serious reflections does this most undoubted truth excite! How cautiously, then, should every act be abstained from that could possibly admit of so dangerous a construction, as an implied fear or doubt of the continued attachment and fidelity of our Sepahees.

No political cause for general distrust and apprehension has hitherto appeared. On the contrary, their valour, devotion, and good conduct have been conspicuously great.

Section the Second.

OCCASIONAL DISAFFECTION OF THE NATIVE TROOPS. THE MUTINY AT VELLORE. THE MUTINY AT BARRACKPORE IN 1824. INJUDICIOUS LARGESSES TO THE SEPAHEES.

TEMPORARY aberrations from duty have occasionally occurred in the native army, but never of an alarming or organised description. Such manifestations were confined to the immediate locality of their unfortunate display, and had their rise not unfrequently in some real cause of grievance, totally unconnected with any political or general feeling of disaffection towards the British Government. There has too often been some misconception of orders or intentions; which, when the ferment of passion subsided, has been generally satisfactorily explained, without the state having to make any weak or humiliating concessions, simply, because there was no act repugnant to its good faith.

Errors and acts of precipitation have occurred, both on the part of the authorities and of the native soldiers. The writer will proceed briefly to enumerate the occasions on which the Sepahees of this army have been guilty of serious derelictions of duty. He will likewise offer his opinion where he thinks sufficient temper and discretion have not been exercised by authority. It will be but just, also, to recapitulate those remarkable instances of a rare fidelity and confidence shown by our Sepahees under appalling distresses; and during the pressure of which, every mode of bribery, intimidation, and intrigue was unsuccessfully resorted to by an artful enemy, to withdraw them from their allegiance. Their implicit confidence in their British officers, neither the brutal threats of cruel enemies flushed with transient success, nor the more fearful horrors of the snows of Caubul, could for an instant weaken or disturb.

Armies, like empires, are raised on everlasting foundations, when based on mutual confidence and attachment. Every act, therefore, which tends to destroy this mutual and most confiding trustfulness, is clearly and directly inimical to the best interests of a state. The most imaginative mind would fail to discover any method more calculated to create alarm and invite disaffection, than precipitate suspicions of the loyalty of its troops.

The British subject must have very inattentively read the history and observed the progress of our dominion in the East, who imagines that any measure is trivial and unimportant, which conveys feelings of doubt and uneasiness on the part of rulers, as to the affection and disposition of the native army.

He must be ignorant of the very elements of which this empire and this native army are composed.

Up to this moment, among the 150 millions of our native subjects, there are none in whose hearts so pre-eminent a feeling of loyalty and attachment towards the British Government exists, as in those of our Sepahees. They stand aloof, in a measure, from the population of India. They are more impregnated with British ideas of right and wrong than any other class of our native subjects. In their own persons, they see and feel the physical and moral strength of our system. Of all natives in India, they are the most unlikely to place themselves in opposition to authority.

Men are not encouraged to conspiracy by observing in the fate of others the danger and calamity of such enterprises.

Discontent, turbulence, sedition, mutiny, attempts to organise insurrection, with an obvious or avowed intention of overturning the existing order of things, or of subverting the Government itself, have all their different complexions of guilt, and distinct phases of character. The latter exhibition of feeling, assuredly, the most daring calumniator would not assert as ever having manifested itself on the part of the Sepahees of this army. Discontent, and occasionally mutiny, have undoubtedly shown themselves. In what army have not such unfortunate aberrations occurred?

In that most truly noble and illustrious service, the Royal Navy of Great Britain, fearful and diabolical mutinies have occurred, and are now chronicled in history.

Though nothing can justify, or even extenuate the infamous conduct of men who use the weapons entrusted to them for the preservation of national honour and safety against the very state herself, yet the British navy of those days had manifold and enormous grievances to complain of.

In the last century, towards its conclusion, there are several recorded instances of individual native regiments having displayed a discontented and mutinous spirit; but on all such occasions, legitimate or imaginary grounds of complaint were the sole causes of the outbreak.

Never had those misguided malcontents the temerity to oppose themselves, in arms, to the just and retributive indignation of outraged discipline. In every one of those instances, after a careful perusal of all the circumstances attending their occurrence, the writer is enabled to assert that the insubordination was entirely confined to those battalions in which it first betrayed itself; and in whose bad conduct and subsequent punishment the rest of the army neither participated nor sympathised. Those unsoldier-like manifestations were promptly quelled, and some terrible examples made of the ringleaders.

Nor does it appear that the men on these occasions either ill-treated their British officers or perpetrated any acts of violence. Their conduct was mutinous and bad, but it was a passive and never an armed resistance, such as usually characterises native revolt against immediate authority.

Far different was the mutiny, however, of Vellore, in the Madras army, in 1806.

Though there are horrible features in this lamentable occurrence, inasmuch as the native troops (chiefly the Mahommedans) were guilty of the most murderous treachery, in attacking and putting to death a great portion of the European garrison, together with thirteen British officers, yet, the additional fact is equally well authenticated, that such open revolt and massacre were entirely confined to the garrison of that place.

It is not disputed that the highest authorities were cognizant of the existence of dangerous symptoms, and had been so for some time before; yet lulled into an apathetic and fatal sense of security, they adopted no precautionary measures to allay the ferment in the first instance, nor were they prepared for its vigorous suppression when it assumed a more dangerous and fearful aspect.

Thus they became the victims of their own want of energy and foresight, and were so judged by the home authorities and the impartial historian of those times. The Governor of Madras and the Commander-in-Chief of that Presidency were recalled, and the Adjutant General and his deputy were also directed to return to Europe. These orders are strongly expressive of severe censure upon their measures in this deplorable affair.

On the mere surface it would appear to the cursory observer, that the proposed introduction of a peculiar and distasteful uniform head dress into the Coast Army was the proximate and ostensible cause of all this frightful mischief; but such an idea would be very much at variance with the real facts of the case.

The seeds of this outbreak had been sown by the sons of the late Sultan of Mysore, long before any innovations in the head dress were contemplated by the British authorities.

The mutiny was entirely the result of Mahommedan fanaticism, confined altogether to men of that persuasion, and fostered and instigated by Moslem bigotry. The emissaries were priests and religious mendicants of that faith, and the final tragedy was consummated by Mahommedan villany and blood-thirstiness.

Numberless concurrent testimonies sufficiently prove that this dreadful event (more a religious emeute than, in correct military parlance, a mutiny) originated in the machinations of the sons of Tippoo, who had been so inprudently permitted to reside in almost regal splendour at Vellore, the scene of their former independent glory, and subsequent humiliating change of fortune.

The pensions of these princes were also on a most profuse and unwise scale, and no concession could have been more faulty than the tacit recognition of their affectation of kingly state and dignity on the very spot of their dethroned greatness, and amidst a population once their subjects.

The infatuation of such procedure was made manifest in the blood spilt at Vellore.

The mutineers, almost all Mahommedans, were of the same religion as the princes, and a greater portion of them old soldiers and former recipients of the bounty of the dethroned family.

The members of this fallen dynasty immediately on this occurrence were removed to Calcutta, where indeed common prudence and policy should have fixed their residence some seven years previously, or immediately after the fall of Seringapatam in 1799.

This fanatical rising was effectually subdued by the slaughter of about 400 of the wretched miscreants, who rose in their support.

Honourable mention is made of a regiment of Madras Native Cavalry which co-operated with the 19th Dragoons in quelling this wild outbreak.

In an article of the *Edinburgh Review*, vol. 18, page 392, referring to the gallant conduct of the native troops at the battle of Assye, the following remarks occur in connection with the particularly firm and resolute behaviour displayed by the above regiment on this very trying occasion: "A more arduous task awaited the latter when the battalions of native infanty which formed the garrison of Vellore were led by the infatuation of the moment to rise upon and murder the Europeans of that garrison. The fidelity of the native cavalry did not shrink from this severe trial, and after the gates of the fortress were blown open, their sabres were as deeply stained as those of the European dragoons, with the blood of their misguided and guilty countrymen."

The results of the numerous investigations following upon this melancholy catastrophe, proved with a lamentable accuracy that scarcely any friendly personal intercourse subsisted between the European officers and their native comrades. A fatal and unwise estrangement divided them. To this may justly be attributed the secrecy with which the plot was arranged and consummated.

It is so clearly the duty and interest of the British officer to cultivate an urbane and conciliating deportment with the native officers and soldiers, that one would conceive it must be strikingly obvious to the most callous and unthinking mind.

Had this happy state of mutual good feeling reigned in the unfortunate garrison of Vellore, it is not too much to affirm that either this hellish plot would never have ripened into maturity, or must have been crushed in the bud. Viewing the subject in this light, how sacred appears the obligation on the part of the British officer to acquire the confidence and attachment of the native soldier.

In November, 1824, a frightful event occurred at Barrackpore near Calcutta. A regiment of native infantry was ordered to the Burmese frontier. Government neglected to provide the requisite means of transport for the families and baggage of the men, who reasonably urged the utter impracticability of moving under such circumstances. The service was of no pressing exigency; a few days delay to have enabled the necessary carriage to be collected could have been of no possible detriment.

The regiment was sternly and peremptorily ordered to march. In consequence of the above difficulty they refused to obey. Unfortunately a transfer of officers had just occurred, consequent to the new arrangements whereby the battalions had been formed into separate and distinct regiments. The European officers posted to this doomed corps were therefore necessarily perfect strangers to the men and without their confidence. Salutary moral control can only be exercised by those possessed of personal influence. With soldiers it is the talisman of command. On this melancholy occasion the British officers from unavoidable causes most unquestionably possessed it not. If they had, what a scene would have been avoided, what carnage would have been spared.

The general officer commanding the presidency division of the army, an amiable but weak man, supremely ignorant of the character and language of the Sepahees, was deputed to harangue them in English; from the perfect ignorance of each others' speech nothing satisfactory followed. What other result could have been reasonably anticipated from such mockery?

A head-strong man was the chief military authority in those days. Unreflecting passion was mistaken for firmness, weakness for energy. The safety of the British Indian empire was perilled that day by the insane violence of a little mind, unconscious that here it would be wise to triumph without bloodshed.

A battery which had been brought up from Dum-Dum was placed in masked position, so that these misguided men had no intimidating conception of the power and determination to enforce submission. The guns, loaded with grape, opened with terrific effect at point blank range.

The regiment was broken, and an indiscriminate massacre ensued; by-standers, innocent and peaceful subjects, allured to the spot by a fatal curiosity, and even some domestic servants of Government House, were involved in one wild slaughter. All the muskets of this ill-fated regiment, when picked up, were found unloaded.

Thus, by a hasty and impolitic act, carried into execution with a fierce and inconsiderate rapidity, was a regiment swept from the face of the earth, which by the exercise of a small share of wisdom might have been reclaimed to a proper sense of duty, and preserved for the future honour and benefit of the British nation.

On all occasions of mutiny and insubordination, that calm inquiry which precedes conviction, and the inevitable punishment solemnly following in the persons of the ringleaders and most guilty, inspire wholesome lessons of awe and dread. Whereas, indiscriminate and wholesale severity, whilst it completely destroys the efficacy of example, confounds every recognised principle of justice.

The whole affair was strongly condemned and censured in both houses of Parliament, and stigmatised by all the journals of the day as rash and impolitic. There was but one voice of condemnation throughout the British empire.

That calm discretion which weighs and examines into circumstances, which decides only upon the most absolute proof or irresistible presumption, and does not punish except on deliberate conviction, which inspires veneration for the majesty of justice by the glorious spectacle of supreme authority armed with the thunderbolt of conscious power, and yet exercising a wise and God-like forbearance, was at this cruel juncture entirely wanting.

For here there was no momentous crisis paramount to all deliberation, where the characters of treason and revolt were so conspicuously manifest as imperatively to demand immediate action, not investigation,—where the urgency of prompt recourse to force was so positive and unerringly apparent that to hesitate was to court destruction.

The danger which was so needlessly apprehended, there were sufficient means at hand to have averted; a pause here would have been the strength of mercy. Discipline was not morally avenged, but morally weakened by the general and dangerous sympathy expressed for those who had suffered a fate so grievously heavier than the nature of their offence merited or justified. Such fearful acts are most injurious to the interests of the State; they involve the innocent with the guilty, and include in one sweeping implication of guilt a numerous body of men, on the ground of general suspicion. Justice cannot tolerate such deeds, and every principle of a wise Government must condemn them The fidelity of no army, however pure and staunch, could stand many exhibitions of such marked mistrust.

The moral fortitude required of a man in a high station of command is a calm, dispassionate, and reflecting fortitude. It is not a passion—it is not a sentiment—it is not precipitation.

Guided and controlled by an enlarged knowledge of the human heart, a just perception of the times and the circumstances, and their obvious and only just requirements, it ever acts with firmness and dignity, and never assumes the awful responsibility of adopting a decided course, of which it has not estimated the tendencies and calculated the effects.

Beyond a general allusion to them, it would

be invidious to speak of the insubordinate manifestations of later years.

One feature presents itself in all of them, grievance on the score of extra allowances withdrawn; and in most cases, the orders and intentions of Government negligently and imperfectly explained to the Sepahees,—in some instances altogether uncommunicated.

In these unhappy displays, disgraceful as they were, it does not appear that the men ever advanced to the commission of overt acts of violence, or presumed to offer more than a passive opposition. Nor were the ramifications of any general organised conspiracy against authority detected. This bad feeling was invariably limited to the scene of its primary ebullition, and was always one of mere selfish cupidity, untainted by any other causes of disaffection. It is gratifying to observe, that on all these occasions native troops, like good and faithful subjects and soldiers, unhesitatingly aided in the suppression of such symptoms, and never for an instant faltered between duty and affection. (To reserve the suppression of such outbreaks for European troops alone would be a fatal error).

Recent general orders abundantly confirm the above assertions, as likewise the startling fact that commanding officers of native regiments have in too many instances shrunk from the duty enjoined them, of preparing the minds of their men for the equitable and indispensable suspension of the extra allowances that they were then enjoying.

The most perversely obstinate and stolid mind is more or less human, and amenable to reason and conviction. The Sepahee is neither brutishly obstinate nor stolid, but, like all other beings, more easily led than driven. The bayonet and balled cartridge are better arguments for enemies in the field than for our own troops labouring under temporary infatuation, and who do not presume to offer an armed resistance: but whenever the infatuation proceeds to that extent, or they refuse to ground their arms when directed, then unquestionably there is no other alternative than to treat them as declared enemies of the state. The following rational views, if they had been calmly explained, must have carried influence and conviction, and would have preserved the honourable character of the native army from being tarnished by many recent exhibitions of a grovelling cupidity: — that the causes which originated and justified the bestowal of extra allowances, no longer existed to sanction their continuance, that such a scale of lavish expenditure could not be persisted in without vast injury to the public finances—without manifest injustice to the people of India, who were as much entitled as its army to the paternal consideration of the British Government; and, perchance, even to the ruin of those noble institutions which provide support for old and meritorious veterans, for all suffering by the casualties of the service, and the advantages of which are available to the impartial participation of every good and deserving soldier.

But, that the display of an ungrateful, base, and reluctant disposition to yield to imperative circumstances with cheerful and instantaneous obedience, was ill-calculated to excite future similar *spontaneous* liberality on the part of a government, both considerate and *discerning*. Unquestionably it is a difficult office to explain to uneducated men measures of state policy, especially when they affect pay and allowances; and a still more delicate task to convince them of their absolute necessity; as also, that the same justice which had so generously and thoughtfully bestowed extra allowances under a peculiar condition of things equally ordained their cessation, whenever a wise and beneficent government recognised their duration as incompatible with the public good, and opposed to the very principles of that justice which had dictated their grant in the first instance as a temporary indulgence.

The simple fact alone of a duty being difficult and delicate should stimulate every exertion of tact, energy, and firmness to accomplish it. To abandon the attempt on the plea of its difficulty is a poor subterfuge to evade the confession of irresolution and weakness. Of late years it has been the fashion to over-pay, over-caress, and over-laud the Sepahee—it is an error, and the fruits are beginning to appear. Unless the system is altered, from being the best he may eventually become the very worst of mercenaries. The idea of our inability to do without him is so perseveringly and significantly presented to his mind, that the perception of his equal, if not greater want of us is obscured if not altogether obliterated.

His "modest stillness and humility" under this storm of inflated eulogium and extra allowances are most astonishing, and honourable to his moral sobriety.

The heartburnings and political embarrassments, moral and financial, which have attended these hasty bestowals of largesse on the native troops are no secret.

The inevitable sequel of such profusion was clearly foreseen and foretold at the time by many officers of practical knowledge and experience of the Sepahee character.

But there appeared to be a competition between some of our rulers for *prætorian* popularity. It is but just, that those who originate such dangerous and extraordinary boons should be obliged to remain on the scene of their triumph and effect their resumption; as the imposition of such an invidious duty on a successor is repugnant to every idea of equity and fair play. To what other motive can the Sepahees attribute these most unlooked-for and gratuitous acts of generosity than to a secret apprehension of themselves? This conviction is palpably forced upon their reasoning faculties when observing an ostentatious liberality displayed towards themselves during an expensive war, and with an empty exchequer. They did not require it, and would have performed their military duties to the State as well, if not better, without it.

To bribe soldiers to do their duty is literally to purchase their honesty and throw it to the winds!

Unmixed cupidity and pride of mind cannot exist together, the stronger passion subdues the weaker, and yet pride of mind is the very essence of all military virtue.

If cupidity be the only feeling worth appealing to when addressing Sepahees, then the riches of the world would be insufficient to satisfy their desires. There is no limit to the insane cravings of avarice.

An improper interference with the long established pay and allowances of the Sepahee would not be a whit more dangerous and impolitic than an unwise increase of them. The pressure of extraordinary circumstances has always been most liberally responded to by Government, a fact acknowledged and appreciated by the native soldier himself. As a general principle, a more docile and well behaved man than the Sepahee of the Indian army does not exist in the world, but he must be kept to his work, and on his *present* scale of *wages*, for he will not stand being pampered without serious deterioration, more than any other human being.

The British Sepahee bears an excellent and respectable reputation in the estimation of the whole population of India, and among them, his inviolable fidelity and attachment to the Government, form a constant theme of remark and unalloyed commendation.

The moral effect produced by this general and salutary conviction of the unswerving devotion of the native army is discerned in the happy and continued tranquillity which reigns throughout India.

It is almost unnecessary to observe that the effect will not outlive the cause.

Section the Third.

FIDELITY OF THE NATIVE ARMY EXEMPLIFIED IN THE MYSORE CAMPAIGNS. OPINION OF WARREN HASTINGS. EXPLOITS OF GODDARD'S COLUMN. MONSON'S RETREAT. THE AFGHAN DISASTERS. LORD MORNINGTON ON THE NATIVE ARMY. NECESSITY FOR A GRADUAL REFORM.

In January, 1757, the first regiment of Regular Native Infantry was raised, since which period, until the present time, embracing a lengthened space of near one hundred years, the character of the native army has remained unchanged in its honourable traits of loyalty and devotion, together with gallantry and good conduct in the field.

It is not intended to give a summary of the distinguished war exploits of the native army, during a whole century, but simply and briefly to refer to those conspicuous occasions, on which the most enduring *fortitude* and *fidelity* were evinced under circumstances of extraordinary hardship, privation, and temptation.

In the wars with Hyder Ali of Mysore, and his son Tippoo Sultaun, commencing in 1767, and with occasional interruptions, only finishing with the fall of Seringapatam, in 1799, the Sepahees of the native army afforded numerous noble proofs of their fidelity and devotion, especially in the memorable and heroic fight made by Baillie's detachment in 1780, against the whole army of Hyder Ali. This small force was literally cut to pieces, disdaining all overtures of the enemy to save their lives by the desertion of their colours and British officers. The same may be said of Braithwaite's small force of 2,000 men (only 100 being Europeans), which contended with noble firmness for two days against 30,000 men, led by Tippoo in person, aided by M. Lally with 400 disciplined French Infantry. During these wars it is remarkable that the enemy possessed most accurate and immediate intelligence of every intended movement of the British, whereas the latter were grievously deficient in this particular and suffered as grievously in consequence.

The crowding in of the camp followers, and its paralysing effect upon the movements of the troops, are commented upon by all the historians of those wars.

Dirom, in his account of the operations of Lord Cornwallis' army, in 1791-92, speaks of these evils, and describes the scene as conveying the idea of a nation migrating, escorted by its troops.

In both of these respects things do not appear much improved even at the present day. Our intelligence department is always most lamentably and notoriously defective, and the followers are usually quadruple the number of the fighting men.

The two following extracts are from Warren Hastings' Narrative of the Insurrection, which occurred in the province of Benares in 1781 :—

"On my arrival at Chunar, I found myself in great and immediate distress for want of money. The troops were some four and others five months in arrears ; and, as the Rajah, Cheyt Singh, had the country on all sides at his devotion, I had not the smallest prospect of obtaining supplies, until the motions of our troops from different quarters should open a communication : I have, however, great pleasure in testifying that, distressed as the sepoys were for the want of money, they never manifested the least symptom of discontent. I frequently visited the camp, and passed the line each time in review : once, and only once, I heard one or two voices of complaint, but neither clamorous or disrespectful."

"The same spirit animated every officer of every corps, and infused itself into the men under their command, with an effect so far exceeding the common occurrences of human affairs, that in the short space of one month, this great and valuable province, which had been suddenly and wholly lost, was in substance wholly recovered to the British Empire."

At this critical emergency, every attempt was made by the Rajah and his emissaries to corrupt the fidelity of the Hindoo portion of the native troops, by solemn appeals to their sense of religion, and regard for the character and position of the Rajah himself, as chief of the holy city of Benares; but to no purpose, nor was their severely tried fidelity for one instant shaken.

The Sepahees shewed great fortitude throughout the campaign in Guzeerat, and against the Maharattas, from 1778 to 1784. The successful and brilliant career of Goddard's detachment, consisting of 4,500 men, which marched from the banks of the Ganges to the western coast of India through hostile and then unknown regions *(clogged, and embarrassed by a select committee of field deputies)* and which performed most astonishing feats of arms,—the taking of the Fort of Gwalior by escalade being one of them,—is the most splendid episode in the Military History of India.

During Monson's retreat in the rainy season of 1804, the fidelity and fortitude of the Sepahees were severely and cruelly tested and heroically proved. In this gloomy and calamitous affair never did the character of the Sepahee shine out with greater lustre. With any other leader it would have been an advance, and not a retreat. Their greatest misfortune was their commander.

The chivalrous devotion of the handful of troops, which in 1817 added lustre to the British name by the successful defence of the Nagpore Residency against an army, has crowned itself with an immortal wreath of glory.

In that painful and most unmitigated of all British military reverses, the flight from Caubul in the winter of 1842, the unfortunate Sepahee did not forsake his colours or his British officer, but nature forsook him.

In a foreign and inhospitable land he perished miserably but without dishonour.

The Sikh campaigns have still further established the fidelity of the Sepahees. It is questionable whether the returns of any army would exhibit such few desertions as occurred in the armies of the Sutlej and Punjaub, during two campaigns, and throughout both of which every specious description of bribery and cajolery was ineffectually played off against the stubborn honesty of the Sepahee.

It may not probably be very generally known, that the Sepahees of the native army had the honour of contributing voluntary subscriptions towards the expenses of the war between England and France; the following general order issued by direction of Lord Mornington (afterwards Marquis of Wellesley) then Governor General of India, confirms this most honourable and interesting fact:

" GENERAL ORDERS BY THE COMMANDER IN CHIEF.

"*Fort William, 23rd November*, 1798.

" The Commander-in-Chief, having received the orders of the Right Honourable the Governor-General in Council, to express to the officers, non-commissioned officers, and private soldiers of the several European and native corps serving under this Presidency, his cordial approbation on the occasion of their voluntary and patriotic contributions towards the support of His Majesty's Government, can in no way so well fulfil the gratifying duty assigned to him, as by publishing the sentiments of His Lordship in Council, in General Orders, to the end that the distinguished testimony which is borne to the zeal and public spirit of the European officers and soldiers, and to the fidelity and attachment of the native troops to the service of the Company and the British Government, may be as public as it is merited and honourable.

"He desires that particular pains may be taken to explain to the native troops the sentiments of approbation entertained by the Right Honourable the Governor General, at the forwardness manifested by them to join their officers in so laudable a cause.

"The Right Honourable the Governor General in Council requests that the Commander-in-Chief will be pleased to express to the officers, and non-commissioned officers, and privates of the several European and native corps, his cordial approbation of the zeal and public spirit which they have manifested in voluntarily contributing a portion of their respective incomes towards the support of his Majesty's Government; and that it will afford to his lordship the greatest satisfaction to communicate to the Honourable Court of Directors so honourable a testimony of the loyalty and liberal disposition of the European officers and soldiers, and of the fidelity and attachment of the native troops to the service of the company and to the British Government."

This pleasing fact alone obliterates a multitude of *petty* indiscretions, and should for ever enshrine the native army in the generous affections of the British nation. This was a very wise and politic appeal to the sympathy of the native army; for nothing can be better calculated to consolidate our power in India than persuading the natives to identify themselves with all the splendid philanthropic improvements of the British Government, having for their object the moral and social regeneration of Hindustan.

We must sink the conqueror in the benefactor. Supported by the aid of the moral and mental sympathies of the people of India, the British empire in the East is invulnerable to the hostile agencies of combined Europe.

Our danger will never be from without, but from within. Though nationality cannot be said in its proper signification *ever* to have existed in India, yet this country has been fertile in revolutions and formidable confederacies. The passions of religious bigotry work strange marvels.

The native army, at present, is distinctly a mercenary, and by no construction can it be viewed as a national one; in fact, it is palpably arrayed against such a spirit. When all the manifestations, on the part of the whole population of India, incontestably evince a most ardent desire for the prosperity and permanency of

British rule, evidenced by a cordial identification with all its measures of policy and amelioration, then this moral deficiency of nationality will be supplied by a feeling akin to patriotism.

Our present greatest safety is our native army, and yet it might become our greatest peril.

The triumph of changing this *mercenary* army into a *patriotic* one is yet reserved for the wisdom of our legislators.

To quit this digression and resume the first subject of discussion; it is hoped, that the insubordinate displays of the native army, since its formation to the present time, have been fairly though cursorily treated; its deeds of fortitude and fidelity set down in an impartial spirit; and that the result establishes a vast predominance of good. Panegyric of the native army is neither required, nor is it the object of the writer.

He believes that the native army is *much* in need of reform, and is susceptible of it; and that it will have to contend with far sterner elements than those it has hitherto opposed and vanquished; and that to meet them with every prospect of success, its moral and physical organization must be more highly *educated* and *improved*.

There are times when reforms are safe, expedient and practicable; others, when their introduction would be attended with danger, and such as nothing but rashness itself would prescribe.

It is conceived by the writer that the favourable period has arrived of effecting a gradual and general improvement of the native army. As the Government of this country is most essentially military, every effort should be exerted to improve the discipline, tone and character of the Sepahees. It is the involuntary *conviction* of our military strength to crush summarily all insurrection, that now maintains peace throughout the continent of India; consequently, as the moral and physical character of the native army progresses, so in an equal ratio will its reputation become further exalted in the general estimation of the whole world. The circle of this *conviction* expands, and it is an expansion of salutary awe and dread.

Weakness, not strength, provokes hostility, and invites the invader.

Section the Fourth.

PASSIVE TEMPERAMENT OF THE HINDOO SOLDIER. HIS PHYSICAL INFERIORITY. A MERCENARY ARMY SHOULD BE ALWAYS EMPLOYED. PEACEFUL LABOURS OF EUROPEAN ARMIES. CASTE PREJUDICES FOSTERED BY THE THOUGHTLESSNESS OF THE BRITISH OFFICERS. CAMPS OF EXERCISE.

THE Hindoo soldier possesses abundantly that calm passive temperament, termed *sang froid;* but, by culture he may be made to acquire the more valuable quality of aggressive valour, and this is the quality which will be required to contend with European foes, and for which contingency, his moral and physical organism *must* be raised. In these attributes the Mohammedan is far superior to the Hindoo Sepahee. The former eats and spends his pay, the latter starves and saves it.

A careful medical inspection of native regiments would fully corroborate this assertion. The institution of monthly health inspections of corps would be instrumental in vastly improving the physique of the Sepahees, by forcibly inculcating the importance attached to the healthy condition, and muscular developement of a soldier. It would give a turn for the practice of those exercises which are best calculated to form a soldier for the duties of his profession, and thereby improve his moral and physical powers of endurance. The acquisition of these powers would necessarily impart the honest pride and feelings of a soldier. He would *properly* respect and *individualise* himself, instead of at present merely looking upon himself as one of the mass which receives eight rupees a month. The Sepahee of the present day possesses in a deteriorated degree that military ardour and spirit which distinguished the native soldier of former times. His cupidity has been inordinately excited, to the decrease of his military virtue and physical efficiency. These medical inspections would operate very beneficially. The state pays most liberally to possess soldiers stout in heart and limb, and not for uniformed anatomies.

It must have struck the most unobservant, the physical lethargy with which the Sepahee handles his musket, and goes through the motions of the manual and platoon exercises. This deficiency does not arise so much from his being overweighted with a piece, which is allowed to be unnecessarily heavy, but from other causes; among them may be mentioned the extent to which hidden disease exists in the ranks of the native army, and to a spirit of increasing apathy.

The greater proportion of the Hindoo soldiers of the native army do not spend above one rupee eight annas monthly in food. How is it possible that the animal stamina can be preserved on such an impoverished diet? We cannot force him to eat, nor would it be politic to interfere with his individual right of doing with his pay as he pleased; but a few examples of men discharged by the medical inspector, as physically unfit, from being in a state bordering on atrophy, would very soon alter the complexion of things. What a provident and wise care is invariably bestowed on the preservation of the health of the European soldier! And yet this important subject as it regards the Sepahee, has scarcely awakened a thought, though he is weighted with the same arms and accoutrements, and even severer duties exacted of him. It cannot be that because the Sepahee is a native of the country, he does not require this supervision, for we observe as a principle the same care and proper precautions adopted towards the European soldier in the mother country, as here.

In fact, it is part of a wholesome and beneficent system that has not yet been extended to the native soldier.

The military tone, and individual physical force of the native soldier, susceptible of melioration, must be attended to and improved, if we indulge the hope that he is to be brought into the field at some future day, to contend with a reasonable prospect of victory, against hardier and far more formidable foes than those he has hitherto been accustomed to combat.

There are no public institutions in existence supported and encouraged by Government for the proper instruction of the native soldiers in athletic exercises, whereby the animal body may be brought to the highest state of physical perfection it is capable of, and the mind strengthened and exalted by the conscious possession of a healthy and superior bodily organism. Such consciousness would unquestionably impart additional courage and confidence of success when in actual conflict with an enemy.

It is imagined that there can be no question but that the state of feeling and *efficiency* of the native army should obtain a paramount share of attention, and at all times excite a serious and wise anxiety: for, upon its agency, attachment, and good conduct must depend the happiness of millions, the safety of our Eastern empire, and indeed, the continuance of that proud eminence which Great Britain now holds among the nations of Europe. This empire has been acquired by the sword, and it is not, and cannot be preserved by the mere efficacy of civil rule, be it ever so wisely or energetically administered. This self evident fact it is presumed no one disputes; and yet, apparently, the army obtains but a secondary and disproportionate consideration. The political importance of the native army is manifest and great, and can never be undervalued with safety. Every thing betokens that the British nation has a still higher destiny to fulfil in the East; and yet it is surprising what very little interest is evinced by the mother country in the affairs of this wondrous empire. There is a pithy adage, that "we never know the value of a thing till we have lost it."

The writer sincerely believes that the period has arrived when this enormous standing army of mercenaries should excite the most serious reflections: and he proposes, without the pretension of arrangement, to unfold his own views on the subject. He is not so presumptuous as to imagine that they will be received without opposition, nor so sanguine as to anticipate for them much attention. His object is to effect good; but should no good accrue from the perusal of his opinions, he still believes that no evil can arise from their widest diffusion.

The campaigns of the Sutlej and of the Punjaub have furnished lessons sufficiently *expressive,* and which experience admonisheth us not to despise. Much can, and therefore *should* be done to improve the *morale* of the native army. Are quadrupeds the only animals which require careful training to qualify them for tasks of pluck and endurance?

A soldier must be in training all his life, and unlike the professed pugilist, never be caught out of condition either morally or physically. The establishment of Government schools of gymnasia; the speedy hearing and adjustment of a Sepahee's civil suits; and the formation of a distinct police force, whereby the employment of Sepahees on anomalous, unmilitary, and, at times, degrading duties would cease, are subjects worthy of a wise consideration.

The organization of such a force would admit of regiments of the line being kept on an *effective* and military footing, which is far from being the case at present. It would facilitate instruction in military exercises and duties;

secure a more close and wholesome European supervision; and elicit and strengthen that amicable community of feeling and interests which it is so desirable should invariably subsist between the Sepahee and his British officer. For in the absence of this bond of union, personal attachment to his officer, with unflinching fidelity to the State, cannot reasonably be expected of the native soldier. The formation of this police force must necessarily keep regiments full and effective; and as it is a well known fact that nothing is more ruinous to discipline, or destructive of the character and energies of man than habits of idleness, the time of the soldier could be kept fully employed. Military exercises, especially individual perfection in ball firing, gymnastics, and employment on works of public utility, such as military roads and fortifications, should form the substratum of a soldier's physical education.

These public works and military roads, accomplished by the soldiers of the State, would be monuments of glory, entitling them to as strong a claim upon the just consideration of their rulers as the greatest triumphs achieved in the field of battle; and would command the respect and admiration of posterity.

It would be a grand political victory to induce

the Sepahees to identify themselves, morally, with these noble undertakings of a paternal government. The development of this feeling would be the first and most important step towards the conversion of a mercenary into a *patriotic* army.

Such occupations engender a healthy and robust state of body, and infuse an honourable emulation and elevation of mind. History is filled with examples of the patriotic works of public utility achieved by the hands of those conquering bands whose exploits in war and industrious labours in peace have immortalised their renown. Was not the famed Appian Way, 350 miles long, a work of the most stupendous difficulties—the road so broad that several waggons could pass abreast—made by the hands of soldiers? In May, 1800, the French Republican army crossed the Alps. The main body, consisting of 30,000 men, artillery, cavalry, and infantry, with all its *matériel,* defiled over the rugged and precipitous Mont St. Bernard. These brave soldiers, by dint of physical labour, transported their artillery, arms, ammunition, and provisions.

Such resolute fortitude was rewarded with the conquest of Italy. Some two thousand years before, Hannibal, under immeasurably greater difficulties, and opposed by the mountain tribes, had performed this feat, justly reckoned as the most extraordinary of antiquity. His troops are represented to have cut their paths through the solid rocks, and to have conquered, in the teeth of nature, the most incredible obstacles, with a perseverance truly heroic and sublime.

And this was an army composed of the most heterogeneous elements: Carthaginians, Spaniards, and Africans!

In his time, soldiers were iron-limbed, laborious, and simple; they were their own artisans and pioneers; entrenching tools, the mattock, and the spade were as familiar to their hard and horny hands, as the sword and the javelin.

Macdonald and Suwarrow have likewise glorified themselves by the passage of the Alps with armies.

On all these occasions the troops suffered fearful hardships, but rose superior to them. Soldiers in all ages have been inured to labour. The wisdom of experience ordains that such should always be the rule, and one without an exception.

There is nothing degrading in performing one's duty; the order from legitimate and responsible authority directing its execution, should be amply sufficient to every well-regulated mind, and invest it with an honourable importance.

The soldiers of the armies of modern Europe are thus employed; and the natives of India are unquestionably inferior to them in all those moral attributes which give dignity to man.

If, therefore, soldiers in this indisputably far higher scale of civilised humanity, discover nothing humiliating in the performance of such professional labours, it is an odious insult to their honest and obedient industry, not to exact similar military duties from the Sepahees of the Indian army.

Soldiers must indubitably in all things assist the government which supports them, or every principle of mutual obligation would soon become confused and eventually destroyed. Soldiers, exempted in time of peace from such labours, and confined to the ease and indolence of large stations, cannot be expected to prove as efficient as they should be in the field, in time of war. They must be very apt to contract habits of a dangerous character, and to imagine grievances, the usual forerunners of disaffection and conspiracy.

The remedy proposed to avert such contingencies, is the gradual introduction of an organised system of military labour. *A vast standing mercenary army, hired by contract to perform the military service of a foreign conqueror, and existing in a state of comparative idleness, might not be dilatory in acquiring a conception of its physical supremacy. This would be nothing new in the history of empires. Legionary violence once in the ascendant, that which has been raised by the surpassing toil of a century, might be thrown down in one day.* At present, the fidelity of the native army is, beyond dispute, firm and unimpeachable.

But to ensure the continuance of this state of feeling, the writer believes that the gradual introduction of a new system is *now* required, whereby the moral tone of the Sepahees shall be improved, by giving it a *patriotic* bias.

He sees nothing unreasonable in his suggestións, and therefore hopes that they may receive some attention, be that attention ever so small.

Where prejudices are strong, the soundest arguments fail to convince; experience itself would plead in vain. No doubt, by many these suggestions will be viewed as the chimerical flights of a theorist, rather than the induction of accurate observations drawn from the present state of the native army. The plan will not be popular, for its operation must necessarily entail additional personal trouble in the acquisition of an apparently remote benefit—and it requires some expansion of mind to value the worth of a remote benefit. As little minds abound, it will be imperative to compel these to discipline themselves to measures of such incalculable national advantage, however much their attainment by a systematic progression may appear irksome and revolting. There is no absolute hindrance to the realization of these objects. Obstructions which strike the weak and irresolute mind as insurmountable, quickly vanish under the grasp of energy. A very erroneous idea obtains currency, that the Hindoo Sepahee could object, with a show of justice, that it would be derogatory and contrary to his religion to obey such a requisition. Never was there a greater fallacy, or one better known to the Sepahee himself. Does he not, in contempt of religious bigotry, wear the regimental cross shoulder belts of bullock-hide, which, when saturated with rain or perspiration, impregnate his body with the very essence of bullock-hide? More than this, does he not know, when he dons the British uniform, and in the process of loading, bites off the end of his cartridge, that that very cartridge (the paper of which is manufactured from the vilest rags) is made in the magazines of the state, by the hands of the lowest castes in the scale of Hindoo creation, and whose very proximity is pollution? He does know it; and yet, like a sensible man, he still continues to perform this little feat of dental dexterity, and to appear at his post on pay day, with a very commendable and rigid punctuality. "It is the badge of service." Does he not follow the corpse of his European officer to its last resting-place, and even on some occasions, when the departed was respected and beloved, volunteer to carry it?

Though to attend any funeral rites, constitutes an obligatory act of three days' fastings and purifications, by the Dhurrum Shastar, or Hindoo moral and social formulary! He is perfectly well acquainted with all this: and yet he returns from the ceremony, doffs his uniform, and, in a cheerful and unmortified mood, proceeds to cook and eat the dinner which the liberal pay of the British Government has enabled him to provide for his creature comforts.

But why multiply similar examples, to prove that by *no* construction can any forfeiture of caste follow the performance of worldly duties or professional obligations. It may appear ungracious and startling to say so; but I have long been of opinion that it is the European officer himself who has mainly contributed to foster this *false* pride of caste frequently affected by some Sepahees. Instead of endeavouring to elevate the mind and character of the native soldier to a British standard of manliness, the officer too often yields to his ridiculous vagaries and unjustifiable scruples, erroneously conceiving that they are the peculiarities and privileges of race. Whereas, that which some officers are apt to view as a decided evidence of high caste, is merely the palpable betrayal of a lazy, ungrateful, and ignoble disposition; indeed the lower the caste, the greater the fastidiousness simulated on such occasions.

It is maintained that wherever the European officer has evinced a zealous and proper professional spirit, the Sepahee has never been found wanting. Good example on the part of the officer is the very soul of military efficiency. There is good authority for asserting that during the arduous siege operations before Mooltan, the Sepahees invariably worked in the trenches with a becoming cheerfulness and soldierlike alacrity. Indeed, there is not one authenticated instance on record of Sepahees having ever demurred to perform such duties when required of them. It is satisfactory to know that their meritorious behaviour in the late campaigns, when performing, like good soldiers, incessant fatigue duties of a very harassing character, has met with the approving appreciation of those best authorised and qualified to form and pronounce judgment on the subject. *A jealous and narrow mind is ever prone to institute false and invidious comparisons, with a reckless disregard of all correct data. The morbid prejudices of these individuals lead them to insinuate doubts of the zeal and good conduct of others; happily for the general weal, this contracted spirit is limited to a few. These unhappy few, however, appear ignorant that it is far easier to inflame bad passions than to create a noble emulation; those who attempt the former are very unlikely persons to be either instrumental or successful in exciting the latter.*

There can be no question as to but one general feeling of esprit de corps existing in the armies of the three presidencies, and when the requirements of the service may combine the troops, that the same impulse of ardour and devotion will proudly animate the whole.

The Government of India supports a most enormous army on a scale of munificent remuneration elsewhere unknown. It gives in a bountiful spirit, and has the right to exact commensurately.

The army is in arrears of civil labours to the Government. By civil labours, is meant those important duties in time of peace, which every Government has a just right to exact of its soldiers.

Butchering the enemy in the field is not so glorious an occupation as assisting in the construction of those great works of public utility, which are to ameliorate the condition of our fellow subjects, and give happiness to countless generations to come.

If the peace of the European world remains undisturbed, except by those brief and occasional interruptions of concord which must, from the inherent faultiness of human nature, be anticipated, (and the bitter maxims of dear-bought experience, together with the progressive wisdom, virtue, and philosophic temper of the age permit this belief and hope), could or would the state maintain so vast a military array for mere purposes of evolution and fruitless display? It is a favourite figure of speech. "We have not troops sufficient —the lower provinces are denuded of troops."

Why, what is the worth of those provinces if they can only be kept in a peaceful, loyal, and productive state by the continued presence of a large military force, the maintenance of which alone absorbs the greater portion of the revenue of those very provinces, leaving but little for the improvement of their social and political condition? If the presence of this large body of military is by the nature of circumstances so imperatively demanded, then the obvious reflection presents itself, as to what advantage has been British legislation in these unwarlike provinces for nearly a century?

The armies of Madras and Bombay have been virtually reduced by detachments from them occupying various posts and stations out of their respective presidencies. This system will admit of still further beneficial extension.

The principle which determines the wisdom of such a measure as respects the withdrawal of troops from Madras and Bombay, one would presume is equally applicable to provinces which have been so long under British influence as Bengal, Benares, and Allahabad. It is true that the anomalous and ill-governed state of Oudh would seem to admit of no cure but the absorption of that country into the British empire, and until this occurs, its misrule and anarchy will continue to exist, but can excite no just cause of apprehension, nor in any degree affect the sound policy of withdrawing troops from a comparatively peaceful locality, and concentrating them elsewhere, according to the nature and obvious exigencies of circumstances.

Nipal is morally, if not physically subdued by the knowledge of our power, and her utter inability to cope with it.

A campaign of sixty days would effectually seal her fate whenever she was so unwise as to provoke and dare the majesty of the British arms. The alarm of denuding the lower provinces of troops would appear altogether visionary.

It is not an immense force which is essential for the preservation of British India, but one, compact, efficient, and elevated by a higher moral impulse than at present influences the Sepahees of the native army. The great captive of St. Helena, in the far-seeing spirit of a master intellect, conceived and forewarned the British nation that the most serious danger they had to apprehend in their eastern empire was the defection of their Sepahee army. It is not unwise to reflect on this prediction, and by every precaution of a grave and prudent foresight to prevent its fulfilment.

May this vast empire, reared with such invincible and gigantic industry, be at least preserved to the great British nation until she has achieved the solemn victory of having rendered it worthy to take its place among the independent nations of the earth!

This would, indeed, be a godlike triumph over the pride of dominion—a sacrifice of moral heroism on a scale of grandeur unexampled in the world's great history!

It may be deemed an officious boldness to touch upon important subjects without strong reasons of necessity; the writer therefore states his honest conviction, that the time has arrived when the *morale* of the native army may be greatly improved, with every facility, safety, and advantage.

A preparation against contingencies is not only a duty, but a necessity; its very neglect may accelerate their approach, though *now* from their apparent remoteness despised, or, still more arrogantly imagined, not within the verge of possibility.

The adage of "let well alone" is altogether inapplicable to the fluctuations and shifting scenes of the human drama, and is an Utopian enigma, if equivalent to anything, equivalent to the calm advocacy of ignorance and imbecility.

In this progressive state, things stationary become immediately retrogressive, and to let "well" alone is simply to smile with a fatuous complacency at making rapid ebb away.

Though the horizon glistens ever so bright and distinct, the wary mariner is neither lulled into a fatal sense of security nor found unprepared when the gale springs up.

The prudence of similar forethought is shown in all mundane affairs.

Whatever precaution gave just assurance of safety against a danger however problematical, even the most insensate mind would not deride its adoption.

The introduction of all new systems undoubtedly requires reflection and caution in their progression. But, if the plan of military labour in time of peace, as now proposed, meets with the approval of the legislative authorities, its gradual and general working may be safely effected with the best moral and practical benefit. The apathy which too generally characterises the British subject in India, were it the national trait, would speedily bring Great Britain, now the foremost nation of all the world, into the same category with Spain and Portugal.

The endurance of military toil in all its forms is comprehended in a soldier's duties; he should be accustomed to do all those things which appertain to military service in tropical as well as in temperate climates, his physical capacities are not unequal to their performance. This is a fact experience has well authenticated.

The plan of military labour is intended to apply equally to the European soldier, as it would be invidious and unjust in the extreme to exempt him from those military toils exacted of the native soldier.

The time of the European soldier in India is not sufficiently employed. The numberless courts martial substantiate this fact. The crimes are those attendant upon his over feeding, and almost listless state of existence. Both his mind and his body are left comparatively without exercise. The common drudgeries of the service are all performed by Sepahees. The European soldier is kept in such luxurious indolence, that it merely requires the addition of a palanqueen to each soldier's stock of necessaries, to render the picture graphic and complete. In the West Indies far more work is exacted of him, to the vast improvement of his health and character. British seamen work with equal moral and physical energy in tropical harbours as in those of *more* temperate latitudes. The value of such labour and exercise is perceptible in their preservation of health and cheerful spirits, with a proportionate absence of crime. The exhaustion in India is more a *mental* than a *physical* prostration; and both are quite susceptible of vigorous preservation by a judicious use of those faculties nature has bestowed on man.

Many of the early campaigns of the Indian Army were made in the rains, and hot months, and yet the troops, both European and Native, kept their health in a remarkable degree. Sickness was almost unknown; the soldiers had not time to be sick. The battle of Plassey was fought in June: the campaign in Guzerat, extending over a period of six years, was carried on during all seasons of the year: the same may be said of the Mysore campaign from 1790 to 1793.

Seringapatam was carried by assault in the month of May. The campaign of 1803 against the Mahrattas opened in the rainy season, and continued throughout, with the most brilliant results. The campaign in Java (1811) was carried on with success during the most unhealthy season of the year. These facts, together with a variety of others all equally well authenticated, are conclusive that so long as the mind and body are kept actively employed, there exists every reasonable hope of the general health of soldiers continuing good and undisturbed, though exposed to all the dangers of a tropical climate during the most inclement seasons of the year. It is more than probable that the troops which served in the above enumerated campaigns would have experienced a far greater mortality had they been subjected to the slothful effects of a cantonment, or barrack life, than they did from actual conflict with the enemy in the field. Greater objection is anticipated by the author to his plan, from the European than from the Native. The realization of such objects must unquestionably entail personal trouble, and personal trouble is abhorrent to an extent in this country which would, if more generally known, excite the derision of our fellow-subjects in Europe.

There is but a very small portion of energy exerted in resisting the enfeebling effects of *example*, the writer will not say *climate;* for he believes that a trifling amount of mental vigour, only properly brought to bear, is always sufficient to modify, if not ward off, its stealthy approach.

Common sense cannot acquiesce in the assumption of an impracticability where no attempt is made to ascertain its feasibility. The exclamation of "what a bore," appears to be the general anathema whenever duty is required. Perhaps there is *no* army in which less duty is exacted from its officers, than from those of the native regiments of the Indian army.

This system of military labour in time of peace can only be put into energetic and effective train by the cordial zeal and *patriotism* of the European officers. Its adoption will give a noble impulse to the native soldier; tend by the diffusion of a patriotic motive to strengthen and secure the British Empire in the East; and redound to the imperishable honour of the native army of India. Surely these are momentous *national* considerations not unworthy the ambition of *British* officers.

In carrying out a system of military labour, *distinct* camps of exercise might be formed and separate portions of work allotted to the different divisions; to be effected under the scientific supervision of the proper officers; by this arrangement, a spirit of ardour and emulation would obviously be excited and fostered.

These camps of exercise would furnish brilliant opportunities of manœuvring the troops on a more extended scale of movement than the circumscribed brigade ground now affords, and over rough and intersected country best adapted to improve all ranks in the practical duties of the field; besides accustoming the troops to scenes and movements more in unison with the realities of war. It would greatly facilitate the acquisition of that confidence and knowledge, the possession of which is so absolutely requisite to enable the superior officers to move large bodies with ease and precision; in its generalising influence, all arms of the service would be greatly benefitted. The operation of this system would necessarily embrace the whole range of military science. The expenses of moving troops might be kept within an economical compass by establishing a system of hiring carriage by *contract*, to meet the necessary and unavoidable changes of ground, whereby its retention on an expensive and permanent footing would be obviated.

There is so much waste land throughout India,

that it is presumed every proper precaution against damage to crops, or loss of any kind to the proprietors of the soil, can always be ensured wherever the troops may be temporarily encamped.

The additional marching batta would be more than covered by the civil labours of the troops, whose military perfection also could not be viewed as an unimportant consideration. From October to March, both months inclusive, these camps of exercise might continue their labours and military exercises.

The grand opportunity would now present itself of effecting those wholesome changes which the imperious urgency of reform demands. Camps circumscribed, followers reduced, baggage curtailed, and all things brought within that simply efficient compass which best beseems the stern hardihood of a British army.

Section the Fifth.

SUPERFLUOUS BAGGAGE OF AN INDIAN ARMY. HORDES OF CAMP FOLLOWERS. SUGGESTIONS FOR A CAMP POLICE. PLUNDERING HABITS OF THE SOLDIERY ON THE MARCH.

EVERY officer who has served in the field must have been struck by the great disadvantages under which an Anglo Indian Army suffers, by being hampered by so much superfluous baggage, and such shoals of camp followers. The existence of these evils unquestionably injures the *morale* of the native army, and is admirably calculated to enervate the minds of soldiers.

Should the Indian army, as at present encumbered with carts, baggage, and infested by its immemorial hosts of private followers, sutlers and packs of human jackals hunting for prey under the mighty shadow of the British banner, ever take the field in Asia, opposed to an enemy aided by a *co-operating European force*, it would require a second army to protect its baggage, stores, and this very scum, against the insults and alerts of such an enemy.

We have not hitherto encountered a truly enterprising foe in India, if perhaps we except Hyder Ali of Mysore, who in 1781 brought the Presidency of Madras to the very brink of destruction. Indeed, such an antagonist would bounteously supply himself from the inadequately protected, and *criminal* redundancy of a modern Anglo-Indian army.

This mob of followers, and frightful train of wheeled carriages are the curse of field movements in India.

A determined energy of resolve would very soon effect a cure. This example of soldier-like simplicity must be presented by the European officer himself, for wholesome regulations should have no respect of person. An Indian camp is a sight ridiculous, preposterous and unmilitary. Every man in it has double what he necessarily requires, and yet he expects that his superfluity is to be protected by harassing the soldiers under his command. Half the baggage might be abandoned without entailing the slightest real personal discomfort. The specific orders of Government, defining the limitation of a soldier's baggage, receive little or no attention. This is clearly the fault of the European officer, who should be held strictly responsible that the

Sepahee on no account be permitted to load more than the regulated weight. At present he moves encumbered with the most unnecessary utensils, and as these necessarily follow in the rear, he looks *backwards* and not *forwards*. "For where a man's treasure is, there will his heart be also," His mind is in a constant state of feverish anxiety respecting their safety. This is not the feeling which should be uppermost in a soldier's heart when on service. It is here that the supervision of the European Company's officer is so much required. For, in respect of overloading, and the transport of useless lumber, the native officers are equally as bad as the Sepahees. They seem quite oblivious to the fact that they render themselves equally amenable to trial for this offence, as for any other subversive of good order and discipline. When orders are reiterated without any satisfactory result, they become so much idle breath, and bring authority into *merited* contempt. This extensive evil can only be eradicated by a strong and inflexible determination. It is a vicious habit which peremptorily calls for *extirpation*. The subject does not obtain one quarter of the attention its importance deserves. Nothing worth accomplishing can be effected without system and perseverance. No detail, though ever so small, should quit the regimental head-quarters without its baggage being most minutely scrutinised, and all surplus articles most unceremoniously ejected. This will beget the habit of marching light on all occasions, and as habit is second nature the most desirable results must ensue. It will affect beneficially individual character in more ways than one, and improve the general tone of the army. A Sepahee by the regulations is only allowed twenty pounds private baggage, whereas, not unfrequently he loads eighty, and certainly rarely less than forty pounds! And the native commissioned and non-commissioned grades in the same proportion of excess over regulation weight. What is the inevitable consequence?

The cattle are overladen, to the ruinous loss of the owners, and to the detriment of the public service—inasmuch as rear guards are most unfairly harassed by this pertinacious disobedience of orders—and, too frequently, baggage thus unavoidably delayed in the rear, is cut off by the enemy, or parties of marauding peasantry. These are, by this success, emboldened to annoy the camp at night, whereby the troops are deprived of their natural repose, and suffer in health accordingly. Camels, which should not carry above

3 cwt., are generally loaded with $5\frac{1}{2}$ to 6 cwt., and in the same ratio with every description of carriage. This easily accounts for cattle knocking up, and their unfortunate drivers deserting. When on detached duties, the Sepahee will never pay for the carriage of his baggage, if he can by any possibility evade doing so. Hence the constant and just complaints from the magistrates of the districts through which these details pass, of their violent acts, forcing porters or cattle to transport their loads, for which they never think of offering payment. On such representations, the guilty party and the officer commanding the detail, ought to be arraigned for oppression and disobedience of orders. Nothing should be left undone to root out this fatal system, and *force* the soldier to march on all occasions as light as possible; his own comfort and real military efficiency are ensured by his so doing.

It often happens that the most serious misfortunes and humiliating reverses arise from apparently very trifling causes.

In that most unnecessary, disastrous, and abject *flight* from Caubul, in the winter of 1841—for at no time, not even on the first day, could it be dignified by the appellation of retreat—the noble efforts of the heroic few, who undauntedly strove to uphold their own and country's honour, were literally paralysed by the heaps of baggage and the crowding in upon them of the panic-stricken rabble of camp-followers, numbering as three to one of that ill-fated band.

But for this legion of locusts, and other lamentable causes, too melancholy to dwell upon, the force, consisting of 5,000 men, might with ease have retained possession of Caubul; or, in spite of adverse circumstances, have effected an honourable retreat to Jellalabad, instead of suffering annihilation at the hands of a cowardly and brutal foe, within the *short space of seven days*.

What a glorious opportunity was there lost, of displaying to the countless hordes of Asia, and to the admiring eyes of Europe, with what unflinching fortitude and successful valour a British detachment could contend against

"The sling and arrows of outrageous fortune."

The formation of an efficient camp police, horse and foot, throughout the service, would prove of inestimable benefit. Whilst in the field, a detail should be attached to every regiment and detachment, and placed under the orders of an European officer; the whole system regulated by a superintendent in chief, and a small capitation tax levied on followers, to defray the expenses of the establishment.

Every camp-follower shonld be duly registered and forbid, under the severest penalties, ever to appear without his pass, which should specify name, caste, personal appearance, occupation, and by whom employed. Without some such stringent regulations, together with an *enforced* limitation of camp followers, baggage, and carriage, the evils will continue to luxuriate, and not improbably, at some future day, entail signal misfortune on the Anglo-Indian army. Detachments and divisions have already seriously suffered from such causes.

The safety, honour, and movements of a field force should be protected against the unbridled license of this rabble, who prowl the line of march in all directions, and commit with comparative impunity, manifold excess, whereby the reputation of the British name is undeservedly wounded and outraged.

The operation of this police supervision would very effectually subdue that organised system of robbery and plunder which tracks the route of British troops through the countries they pass, whether as friends or foes.

One of the secret causes of our imperfect intelligence may be attributed to the personal enmity of the people of the country, engendered by these marauding practices. The march of troops in India is frequently followed by the execrations of the peasantry. The most bold and reckless are goaded into revengeful reprisals. When this occurs, the troops are the chief sufferers in the end.

It is on the occasions of field service that the contractors, by the aid of British prestige and assistance, are so successful in collecting enormous supplies of every description, the greater portion of which is less for the actual provision of the force, than for the exercise of their speculative genius. They realise immense profits.

Indeed, this is the season in which these harpies gather in their harvests, and revel in extortion and villany. Their successful frauds on the Government are of proverbial notoriety.

The efficiency of the regimental bazaars might be greatly increased, if every judicious effort were made to encourage and *establish* a system of cash purchases; and strongly to inculcate on the minds of the Sepahees the obvious advantage to themselves of avoiding the opening of credit accounts with the dealers.

The camps of exercise would bring all these

evils under the salutary influence and control of a reformed system.

Though these suggestions are offered in a desultory form, yet they are not the less on that account entitled to the grave consideration of the higher authorities.

Or, are the evils of such growth, that courage and fortitude are wanting to grapple with them?

Section the Sixth.

THE NATIVES OF INDIA KEPT TOO DISTINCTLY APART FROM THE CONQUERING RACE. GREATER COMMUNICATIVENESS ON THE PART OF GOVERNMENT DESIRABLE. PUBLIC WORKS TO BE CONSTRUCTED BY MILITARY LABOUR. ELEVATION OF THE SEPAHEE.

No salutary reformation, on a grand scale, can succeed, unless those who should be mainly instrumental in its progress, co-operate with unaffected zeal and devotion.

As all improvements, and changes of any sort, are invariably viewed in India with excessive jealousy and dislike, their successful introduction can only be effected by a judicious circumspection, in unison with the peculiar habits, ideas, and prejudices of the people for whose actual benefit they are intended. It has often forcibly struck the writer, that the native mind might be most advantageously appealed to, and enlightened on the subject of those grand philanthropic undertakings in progress, and in contemplation, for the amelioration of their own country.

The conquerors and the conquered still appear in distinct political relievo. The people of India are unquestionably more ruled than governed. So long as cupidity and fear continue to be the only *passions* addressed, so long must the higher motives of human action remain inert and undeveloped. The splendid public works and institutions founded by opulent natives, substantiate that, under the influence of the promptings of the heart, they are capable of great deeds.

Whether originating in bigotry, religion, or a desire for the applause of their fellow-creatures, the merit of such useful actions is great, and deserving of commendation.

A generous confidence and political amenity, displayed towards them by the Government, may gradually induce these tendencies to flow into other channels, and eventually be the happy means of calling forth a patriotic feeling among the population of India. Until such a spirit is awakened, this empire, gained by the sword, must be *ruled* by the sword.

What possible interest can they feel in great social undertakings and improvements, with which their personal identity is neither courted nor anticipated? The identity here referred to is a moral and not a mercenary identity. The identity of the heart.

This feeling might be elicited by the Government communicating to the people of India, through the medium of vernacular notifications, the public objects of all extensive plans of improvement for the present and future amelioration of Hindustan. Such political courtesy would be attended with many advantages—it would greatly conciliate and raise the natives in their own moral estimation—strengthen their allegiance and attachment—and induce them to contemplate the beneficent intentions of the British Government towards themselves in its true and proper light—and finally induce them to associate themselves in their worldly feelings, and interests with the British nation.

The creation of such a spirit would manifestly tend to facilitate all measures of public utility, the institution of which is *now* viewed with undisguised apprehension, as an insidious attack on caste, custom, and religion.

Those who have been dispossessed of power and influence by the inevitable results following on the consolidation of a new empire, and by the operation of a system which is opposed to the admission of natives into offices of political importance, are one and all the most implacable enemies of the British Government.

Native priestcraft (Hindu and Muhammedan) is ever at work to invest with a jaundiced complexion every act of the legislature, communicates to the people the vindictive spirit with which it is inflamed, and makes use of their ignorance and superstition to excite a most obstinate resistance to all measures of a benevolent reform.

This pernicious domination would be effectually undermined by the natives being correctly informed and educated as to the real objects of their rulers. Truth will ultimately prevail over falsehood, however artfully disguised by the machinations of an unscrupulous and furious priesthood, and in the end expose the impure and interested motives of such hostility.

As occasion required, a pamphlet might be drawn up by those best qualified for the task, embodying all the information either necessary or prudent to afford, submitted for the judgment of the highest authorities, and on their final approval, printed in the vernacular.

Copies might then be distributed as school books to the different Government institutions for native instruction, and numerous others disseminated throughout the Peninsula of India.

The extensive promulgation of such disinterested intentions on the part of the ruling powers towards its native subjects would be admirably calculated to excite their veneration and attachment, and operate in crushing the secret workings of hatred and opposition.

The writer believes, and states his conviction, that the circulation of these vernacular political pamphlets would tend much to improve the hearts and minds of the natives of India.

These unreserved communications on the part of a great Government to its native subjects could not but animate them to *prove* that they were worthy of such marks of confidence and esteem.

This is a powerful engine for good that has not hitherto been worked in India.

There is no race in the world more imbued with self esteem than the Asiatic, or whose enthusiasm by tact can be more easily excited and elevated.

Briefly to resume the subject of military labour. It appears to the writer that the newly acquired territory of the Punjaub offers a suitable field for the honourable exertions of the troops. All the military roads of that province ought to be accomplished by them. They should scorn to traverse those not made by themselves. Such labours would remain lasting memorials of the gratitude and devotion of an army, and be a suitable return for the great benefits they and their forefathers have experienced at the hands of a generous and most liberal Government

As some years may elapse ere it would be either safe or even practicable greatly to reduce the numerical strength of the Indian army, intermediately it might be employed in laying down these grand lines of communication from one end of the empire to the other, excavating canals, and assisting in the construction of all those splendid works of public utility so worthy of the philosophical and exalted genius of a powerful civilised government to originate and accomplish.

Among other undertakings now in operation, may be particularly mentioned the Ganges canal, still worked by sordid contract, and menial hands, toiling its weary length along, which would rapidly advance towards completion under the disciplined physical force and energy of 10,000 soldiers, encouraged and animated by the presence and exhortations of their British officers, inspired by a zealous and *patriotic* spirit.

On the final completion of these great public works, lofty obelisks might be raised, (which would also answer for telegraphic and other useful purposes,) to commemorate the names of the different regiments employed, and when in the lapse of centuries these obelisks should be no more, the blessings of posterity would ascend to the throne of the eternal, and on earth history plead against oblivion for the memory of their deeds!

It is clearly impossible for the Indian Government to maintain such an immense military establishment in time of peace without deriving some commensurate return. Its finances would sink under the pressure.

It would be a ruthless and impolitic expenditure of the resources of the empire. They are ordained for far higher purposes—the amelioration of a vast country, entrusted by the Almighty to the care and protection of the British nation, and for which hitherto with the very best intentions so little has been achieved—for the honour and preservation of the British name in the dispassionate estimation of succeeding generations—and lastly, and gravest consideration of all, for the approving judgment of the Great Creator of the universe. Who, in his all-searching and most just spirit will, though requiring a full account of our stewardship, not fail to reward the righteous deeds, and glorious aspirations of a wise and beneficent rule. And may not the hope be reverentially indulged, that these generous and philanthropic labours of a great people for the regeneration of a vast portion of the human race, will in His divine mercy be permitted to weigh in the final redemption of the whole family of man?

This is a solemn reflection not undeserving of the most serious thoughts of a mighty Christian nation!

With every just and sacred regard for the rigid fulfilment of all stipulations of service, and an unvarying conciliatory respect for the religious feelings, customs, *yea*, even prejudices of the Sepahee of our army, we should commence, nevertheless, the introduction of a reformed system whereby he may be morally and physically improved. His mind should be disciplined as well as his body. He must now be *educated* to meet an European foe in the field, and to experience as much military humiliation in turning his back upon a white man, as upon a black one.

If he is unwisely made to repose so implicitly

on the superior energy of his European fellow-soldiers, he will not give his own fortitude and courage sufficient scope and estimation. His military pride has been too frequently wounded by injudiciously isolating European troops on distinct points of attacks, whereby the Sepahee could not fail to perceive that he was viewed in a very secondary light. The display of such marked want of confidence in the prowess of the native soldier, undoubtedly tends to quench his zeal and spirit. He ceases to feel as a soldier. Under the electrifying influence of an heroic chief possessed of *genius*, (that most inscrutable of all gifts,) and professional ability, the ardour and enthusiasm of the Sepahee can be elevated to the highest tension of military exertion. He then feels proudly conscious that he is something more in the estimation of his Commander than an animated target, or senseless automaton merely hired to pull a trigger. Great leaders have ever succeeded in animating the native soldier with their own spirit, and accomplished deeds that any army might be proud of. Where this spirit cannot be infused there must be something morally deficient in the commander, for the Sepahee has proved in abundant instances that the deficiency does not exist with him. To lower the Sepahee of our army in his own opinion, by the betrayal of the slightest distrust either in his attachment or courage, is destructive to every feeling of pride and emulation, and calculated to plunge him into a fatal and hopeless apathy. He ceases to look upon the army as a noble profession, but simply as the channel through which a few sordid rupees may be amassed. His tone and military efficiency is only to be preserved by his British officers taking a sincere and generous interest in his welfare and improvement.

If he has been overlauded by nauseous and indiscriminate panegyric, he has not the less been vilified by an equal share of undeserved disparagement on the part of others, whose ignorance is no excuse for their slander. It is only those who know him best that can fully appreciate his many excellent and soldier-like qualities. It has always been observed that the severest commentators upon men and measures are those the least qualified to pronounce a candid and impartial judgment.

Section the Seventh.

HEROIC EXPLOITS OF SEPAHEE CORPS AT CUDDALORE, AND AT BHURTPORE. THEIR DEGENERACY, THROUGH CUPIDITY.

No man can rise from a perusal of the military history of India without a very high and favourable opinion of the prowess and devotion of the Sepahees. The writer will cite a few examples, among the many which could be produced, for the especial attention of the younger European officers of the native army. Though the writer is sensible of the manifest advantages of combining both European and native troops in all military operations in India, yet there are not wanting numerous instances where a force composed entirely of Sepahees have achieved brilliant results.

But then they were fortunately commanded by leaders of genius and professional skill, who thoroughly understood and appreciated them, and had succeeded in acquiring their unbounded confidence and attachment. Goddard's detachment,* in a most arduous campaign from 1778 to 1784, fought and gained several pitched battles, besides taking by storm many forts and entrenched cities. In this campaign, in the month of August, 1780, Captain—the late Lieut.-General—Popham, with about 2,000 Sepahees, carried the fort of Gwalior by escalade; and such was the nicety of the enterprise that all the Sepahees employed on the occasion were provided with shoes made of strong cloth quilted with cotton. In the following year Lieut.-Colonel Camac, with five battalions of native infantry, a small proportion of artillery, and some native cavalry, surprised by a forced march, the camp

* Six battalions of Sepahees, viz.:

1st, 2nd, 4th, 5th, 6th and 7th. 900 rank and file each	5,400
One regiment Native Cavalry	600
One company's Native Artillery	100
Candahar horse	500
Total fighting men . . .	6,600

With 103 European Officers.

This force was accompanied by followers, servants, and bazar people amounting to 31,000!!!

It commenced its march from Cawnpore in the worst season of the year, during the rains of 1778, and did not arrive at the scene of operation, on the western coast of India, till March of next year.

A considerable time after military operations had commenced this detachment received the addition of a few European companies from Madras; but the pressing exigencies of that presidency required their subsequent recal, as likewise even additional succour from Bengal.

of the Maharattas, and totally defeated the enemy, taking all their *materiel.*

During the wars with Mysore, the Sepahees, on several occasions encountered the French in the field. One remarkable instance mentioned in Orme's History of India, is also briefly narrated in the Encyclopædia Britannica, vol. 5, p. 600. "In 1783, Cuddalore, then in the possession of the French and garrisoned by them, was invested by the British Army commanded by General Stewart. It was during this siege that the enemy formed the design of not only forcing the British to abandon the attempt, but of annihilating them. For this purpose 4,000 men were landed from the squadron commanded by M. Suffrein, and the conduct of the enterprise committed to the Chevalier de Damas, an experienced and valiant officer. On the 25th June 1783, he sallied out at the head of the regiment of Aquitaine, supposed to be one of the best in the French service, and of which he was Colonel, with other troops selected from the bravest of the garrison. The attack was made by daybreak, but though the British were at first put into some disorder, they quickly recovered themselves, and not only repulsed the enemy, but pursued them so warmly that the Chevalier de Damas himself was killed, with about 200 of his countrymen, and as many taken prisoners. This engagement was attended with one of the most remarkable circumstances that happened during the whole war; viz., a corps of sepoy grenadiers encountering the French troops opposed to them with fixed bayonets, and overcoming them. This extraordinary bravery was not only noticed with due applause, but procured for that corps a provision for themselves and families from the presidencies to which they belonged."

In the foreign expeditions against Java and the Isle of France in 1811, the Sepahees again crossed bayonets victoriously with the French troops of the line, whose *amour-propre* was sorely wounded by being pitted against, and vanquished in fair fight by the "black fellows of India." It is related in *all* the accounts of those expeditions, that the Sepahees met the French with the bayonet in the most cool and determined manner. One man most particularly signalised himself at the taking of Java, and his prowess is mentioned in several works. *Williams's Native Infantry* likewise chronicles the exploit. "A sepoy volunteer from the 1st battalion, 27th regiment of Bengal Native Infantry, named Bahadur Khan, who was detached with the flankers, distinguished himself on the day of the action; he certainly bayoneted six of the Frenchmen, and did not fire a shot: some of the Europeans of His Majesty's 69th and 78th say he killed nine. He was promoted to Naick or corporal the next day."

At the first siege of Bhurtpore in 1805—the native troops employed gave astonishing proofs of chivalrous gallantry. The colours of the 2nd battalion, 12th regiment Native Infantry (the present 1st regiment N. I.) were three several times planted on the crest of the breach. Alison in his History, vol. xi. p. 126, records the circumstance, giving official authority for his statements: "The scaling ladders of the party destined to attack the gate were found too short, or were destroyed by the terrible discharges of grape which issued from its defences; and, despite all their efforts, the brave 75th and 76th were forced down with dreadful slaughter from the breach. They were ordered out again to the assault, but the troops were so staggered by the frightful scene that they refused to leave their trenches; and the heroic 12th regiment marched past them with loud cheers to the breach. Such was the vigour of their onset, that the brave Indian soldiers reached the summit in spite of every obstacle, and the British colours were seen for a few minutes waving on the bastion; while the 76th, stung with shame, again advanced to the assault. The bastion proved to be separated by a deep ditch from the body of the place, and the guns from the neighbouring ramparts enfiladed the outwork so completely, that the valiant band, after losing half their numbers, were in the end driven down the breach, weeping with generous indignation at seeing the prize of their heroic valour thus torn from them." This was the effort of the left attacking column under Colonel Don, composed of H.M. 75th and 76th regiments, 1st and 2nd battalions of the 12th regiment, N. I., and 1st battalion 15th regiment N. I. When the Europeans refused to move out of the trenches, the two battalions of the 12th regiment, N.I. were ordered out, and led on gallantly by Colonel Don, and their officers moved out from the right of the new breaching battery, and pushed on to the ditch, accompanied by two 6-pounders, under Lieutenant Swiney, to fire grape at the defences.* All the accounts prove that had the European troops supported these gallant native battalions the place might have been won.

The siege operations before this fortress lament-

* British Indian Repository, No. 5. "Siege of Bhurtpore."

ably illustrate the fact, that it is too much the characteristic of Indian warfare to make valour on all occasions supply the place of science, and the result has been, and ever must be, so long as this fearful contempt of all fundamental military principles continues to increase unnecessarily the wasteful sacrifice of life.

The enemy is generally allowed to take up his own position, and sufficient time is afforded him to strengthen and fortify it. A flank movement is seldom attempted, whereby it may be turned, or his attention distracted, but we go at it with bull-dog ferocity, attacking the strongest part, which is usually defended by artillery. It is at last carried by the gallant survivors literally wading to victory in the blood of their slain comrades. The professional blunders of the commander are quenched in the life streams of the troops.

The following interesting extract from the General Orders issued by Lord Lake, after one of the failures to carry that fortress by assault, will declare the conspicuous heroism shown on that occasion:—" Notwithstanding the distinguished and persevering gallantry displayed by the troops in the assault of yesterday, and that the colours of the 2nd battalion, 12th Regiment, were three times planted on the top of the bastion, the obstacles were such as not to be surmounted."

At this siege, several of the native regiments lost more than half their numbers in killed and wounded. In the "British Indian Military Repository," vol. v., under the article "Siege of Bhurtpore," the following exploit is given :—

"*January* 22*nd*, 1805.—This day, the 1st Regiment Native Cavalry, and 1st Battalion 15th Regiment Native Infantry, were dispatched, under the command of Captain Welsh, of the former corps, for the protection of a convoy of provisions, on its way from Deig to camp.

"*January* 23*rd*.—The convoy, under Captain Welsh, which marched from camp yesterday, joined the Deig and Muttra convoy last night, which consisted of 12,000 bullock-loads of grain; it was encamped last night about 22 miles from camp, and moved towards the army early this morning. Holkar having received intelligence of its approach, and of the nature of the force employed for its security, had detached Meer Khan against it, with his whole army of horse and foot, and four guns. With this force, amounting to 8,000 men, Meer Khan lay in wait near to Combhere (Komeer), and at break of day fell in with the detachment, about six miles from camp. The cavalry of the detachment being only 400 strong, could not protect 12,000 bullocks when marching; and, under these circumstances, the detachment took post in a large village of lofty site, where, beset on all sides, they defended their charge, beating off the assailants repeatedly, till two of their guns were totally disabled. The enemy's horse and foot then making a desperate push, possessed themselves of half the village. Such was the state of things at half-past eight this morning; and, although the firing had been heard early, it was not till near eight o'clock that Lieut.-Colonel Need, with half of the 2nd Brigade of cavalry, hurried by the Commander-in-Chief out of Camp, and hastened in that direction. General Lake, with Colonels Wood, Vandeleur, and Brown, and the rest of the cavalry and horse artillery, following immediately to support. The Sepoys of the detachment perceiving the clouds of dust that marked the advance of Lieut.-Colonel Need's column, raised loud shouts of exultation at the approach (as they fancied), of General Lake, and, under this impression, were so animated as to sally forth upon the enemy's guns, which they carried at the point of the bayonet, just as the cavalry arrived, who, dashing in, covered the ground with killed and wounded before the rest of the troops with the Commander-in-chief came up. Six hundred of the enemy were slain, the rest fled, leaving behind near forty stands of colours, with four guns and their tumbrils." The detachment was complimented and thanked in General Orders for its noble and heroic conduct under these perilous circumstances.

In Monson's retreat, the preceding year (1804), numberless acts of the most devoted valour were performed by the native troops, who implored the commander to stand and give battle; but, lamentable to say, Colonel Monson weakly acknowledged that he had no confidence in such men—soldiers who, when a few months afterwards employed at the siege of Bhurtpore, gave such astonishing proofs of heroism and devotion!

In this miserable running away, persisted in by an incapable chief, and which military courtesy has termed a retreat, the following trait of gallant devotion unto death is related in "Williams's Bengal Native Infantry," Appendix, page 371;—"At the passage of the Banass river, on the 24th August (1804), when the troops composing the rear guard, consisting of the 2nd Battalion 2nd Regiment, and the piquets of the line, under the gallant Major Sinclair, were nearly annihilated by the overwhelming force which the enemy brought against them after the rest of the detachment had crossed the river, and could render the rear guard no support, large bodies of the enemy's horse having also crossed the river to keep them in check, a remarkable instance of heroism and devotion was displayed by a Subadar or Jemadar of the 2nd, who was seen from the opposite side of the river, retiring with a stand of colours in one hand, and defending himself with the other, until he reached the bank of the river, into which he plunged, but sunk with the colours to rise no more." In the Sikh campaigns, their gallantry and fidelity have been as signally tried. Some of the native regiments lost, in killed and wounded, more than half their numbers, and were mowed down in their ranks in as regular order as if drawn up on parade. Whenever European soldiers and Sepahees have been long associated, and severely tried together, our gallant countrymen have never failed to value, and justly value, the dusky warriors of Hindustan.

The writer trusts that he has succeeded in proving to the young officers of the Indian army, that the Sepahee is not only entitled to consideration, but to respect. It is the *duty* of the British officer, and should be his pride and pleasure, to take a deep interest in the honour and welfare of his native fellow soldier.

Though the writer has unquestionably a high opinion of the Sepahee, founded on an intimate acquaintance of twenty-eight years, yet he is not prepared to coincide with the fulsome laudation of injudicious panegyrists.

The writer truly believes that the Sepahee has deteriorated both morally and physically, and that the decay is attributable to the prevalence of a vicious system. The idol of avarice has been raised by those who should have known better, and the Sepahee has worshipped at the debasing shrine until he *recognises* no other worship.

Gold has become his god, under the guise of "extra allowances." His cupidity has been most dangerously excited—it is the first lesson in the formation of a Janisary! The chink of rupees has become more delightful music to his ears than the martial strains of the "Grenadiers' March."

The stimulus connected with an idea of military glory, or of great achievement in war, is never presented to his imagination; in the shape of donatives he obtains the ignoble recompense of a gladiator.

Though the spoils of the vanquished have ever,

by the courtesy of precedent, been awarded to the effective valour of the victor, yet it should recognise no right to the expectation of a bribe in the shape of "extra allowances," for the performance of military duty in a conquered territory, become an integral portion of the empire.

This error, if persisted in, will either prove destructive of all right military feeling in the native army, or at no distant day be effaced by some *terrible scenes.*

There is a limit to forbearance, after which it becomes fatal imbecility. It has been an easy matter to grant that, which it will be found not so easy to reclaim. A bestowal of extra allowances on all occasions of field service is, it must be admitted, a most dangerous and ruinous precedent, and cannot be too soon or too firmly abolished.

There is a vast distinction between a wise foresight, which prevents demand, and that melancholy feebleness which meets it with concession.

It must ever be a difficult and hazardous attempt, after a precedent has been established, to require Sepahees, or indeed any soldiers, to acquiesce in the propriety of its repeal, more especially when it is one that sanctions and concedes *substantial* pecuniary advantages. Soldiers are not formed to reason, but to feel, and to *act* under the ascendancy of feeling. Reduce the emoluments of a mercenary, and his zeal and attachment are diminished in an equal ratio.

Hire is *here* the reward of service, and if the stipulator in the minutest particular vitiates the contract, it is not probable that the engaging party will prove very scrupulous in its fulfilment. There can be no moral permanency of action under the operation of such causes, and yet these are the motives which influence at the present time almost every act of the native soldier. Consequently, every effort should be strained to inculcate a higher tone, and this can only be effected by his European officer zealously co-operating in promoting an object of such manifest importance to the service at large, and from the realization of which the British Government of India must ultimately derive increased strength and stability. Those ties which should connect the Sepahee with his British officer must be drawn closer, that thereby the true interests of the service and of the state may be more effectually and firmly secured. This is a subject from which, of late years, almost all consideration has been withdrawn.

The action of the mind is naturally connected with the physical condition of the body; and in the profession of arms especially, all great and enduring efforts depend on the healthy union of both. With the Sepahee scarcely any attention has been paid to these essential points, and consequently his moral fortitude, and physical powers susceptible of considerable improvement, remain imperfectly developed. It is the fashion to consider him as a child; but a spoiled child, in course of time, becomes a very disagreeable and *mischievous* animal. If he has not inherited these intrinsic qualities from nature, the deficiency must be supplied by an improved professional culture.

This second nature, or habit, cannot be formed without time, and the most zealous assiduity on the part of the European officers, but once engrafted and firmly rooted, the Sepahee can be depended upon under all the various phases and vicissitudes of war.

Some of the finest specimens of the animal man, the writer has observed in the persons of the Bengal Sepahee. Though from natural causes he may not possess that ardent constitutional courage, the birthright of the Briton, and which Cæsar ages since thus characterised—"Valour is indigenous to the British soil;" yet on numberless stricken fields he has proved himself not unworthy to contend in the same ranks with British soldiers.

With proper care and attention the writer honestly believes that the Sepahee would not flinch from battle with any of the troops of European nations. He has shown that he will not recoil from the mercurial intrepidity of the French. The stolid phlegm of the Austrian, Saxon, and Bavarian troops is not calculated to dismay him. The Spaniards or Portuguese would still less disturb his military equanimity.

In mechanical discipline and precision of movement the Sepahee battalions will bear a comparison with any army. The writer speaks from personal observation in making, not hazarding, this assertion.

Notwithstanding all this, a sentiment of military pride and self importance should be kept constantly before his eyes, he must be instructed by his *British officers* that battles are not gained over a daring and resolute European foe by prestige, but by the combination of those military virtues, distinctive of the true soldier. And that when before such an enemy, the cry of "Sirkar ka Ikbal,"* though shouted with all the stentorian strength of a whole line of Infantry, is not worth one determined push of the bayonet.

* Prestige of the State.

Section the Eighth.

THE SIKHS. FOREWARNED, FOREARMED. ENLISTMENT OF SEPAHEES FOR GENERAL SERVICE.

In the late campaigns against the Sikhs, the Sepahees were surprised at the frenzied gallantry with which that truly military race fought for victory; nor were the European portion of the force much less astonished at their stubborn and strenuous resistance.

Never had the Sepahees been so severely tried or called upon to face such astounding batteries —batteries admirably and heroically served, with the additional advantage of being placed in entrenched position, whereby every hope was inspired of ultimate success.

Such conflicts have rarely been witnessed even on the battle-fields of Europe, where valour and strategetic science more equally matched, contend with proportionate pride and obstinacy for the mastery.

It was literally the storming of a succession

of fortresses in the field, bristling with cannon and aided by the galling fire of a numerous veteran infantry protected by raised parapets of earth, and who plied their fire with extraordinary rapidity as the British troops came within musket range. The higher moral incentive to action was likewise on the side of the Sikhs fighting *pro aris et focis*, and *for* salvation against utter political extinction.

Their fall is a moral. Flushed with conquest they scorned the arts of peace, the honest and laborious pursuits of agriculture, and were subdued less by the sword of the Saxon than by their own infatuation, *cupidity*, and *military truculency*.

During these wars, desertion in the ranks of the native army was almost unknown; this is a gratifying and well established fact that cannot be too often repeated. The gold and temptations of the enemy (though Hindoos themselves) had no disturbing effect on the allegiance of the British Sepahees.

The ranks of the Sikh army contained numerous men from the same districts and provinces which chiefly furnish recruits for the Bengal native army. In the regular Sikh army were likewise *distinct* regiments, composed almost entirely of inhabitants of Hindustan proper. The Sikh artillery was usually manned by these foreign drafts. When the hostile armies were drawn up opposite each other for a considerable period preceding the action of Sobraon, the soldiers from both were in the constant habit of clandestinely visiting each other. In these campaigns fathers fought against sons, and brothers against brothers.

It might be urged that the merit of military fidelity was consequently equally divided; not so, for the Sikh authorities offered bribes and promises of superior rank and consideration to our men to desert, and even priced the heads of the different grades of British officers. In fact, every industrious baseness was practised by the enemy to allure the Sepahees from their standards.

As the Sikh army recruited without regard to any regulated height, all those men of our provinces desirous of our military employ, and against whom this objection militated in the British army, experienced no difficulty whatever in entering that of the enemy.

All these circumstances the more honourably enhance the fidelity of the British Sepahees.

Still the writer reiterates that they must be professionally trained to fight and vanquish far more formidable foes, better organised, and held together by immeasurably superior influences than the wild fanaticism of the Sikhs, if they are ever to be brought into stern collision with a disciplined European antagonist.

It is highly probable that the land of Egypt may witness a severe struggle, calculated to affect considerably the question of the supremacy of British eastern dominion, either by decisively exhibiting our strength, or by rendering it necessary to renew the contest on other fields.

Coalitions have been formed against the colonial possessions of great Britain, and may be again. Her enormous power and prosperous fortune are undoubtedly viewed with the most intense and malevolent jealousy by the whole continent of Europe—a feeling in which Russia largely partakes. Would America lament to see her great parent humbled?

That species of equity which expatriated "the most just" of antiquity, is but a type of the political ostracism of modern times.

It would, indeed, be a suicidal and *un-British* act to await supinely the completion of an enemy's plans. Consequently, the first note of warlike preparation on the part of any European power, with a palpable demonstration towards Egypt, should be the signal for our prompt military occupation of that country, which is the very key of our eastern position, and retaining its possession till all danger had passed. There is historical precedent and *sanction* for the act. Illustrated, it simply amounts to this—an enemy rushes forward to dispossess a feeble third party of a sword, wherewith to assail you—your greater activity meets and defeats the movement.

The common instinct of self-preservation demanded and morally justified the precaution.

Previous to the bombardment of Copenhagen and capture of the Danish Fleet, in 1807, all pacific overtures had been bravely though haughtily rejected, and the result was one of vital necessity. Being *successful*, it was a *perfidious* aggression!

James, in his "Naval History," vol. iv., p. 161, thus fairly treats the subject:—"With respect to the expedition to Copenhagen, morally and politically considered, the British public was for a long time divided in opinion. At length, as affairs in the northern part of the continent began to develope themselves, the necessity of the measure became generally admitted, and both Houses of Parliament voted their approbation of the conduct of Ministers on the occasion.* It is not a little singular, too, that the very man whose design it was the object of that measure to defeat, has since declared, that the expedition showed great energy on the part of the British Government." By this energetic stroke, the plans and intentions of Napoleon were entirely frustrated.†

It is not unreasonable to believe that had the ministry of those times not adopted these measures of a wise precaution, their conduct would have subjected them to subsequent impeachment, the condemnation of their country, and the deserved censure of history.

As the occupation of Egypt necessarily infers the existence of war in Europe, and the presentation of many vulnerable points of the colonial empire of Great Britain to the attacks of the enemy and all of which would require to be defended by European troops of the line, it follows as a matter of necessity that a large *native* force must be organised for this expedition. From the nature of the duties involving protection of baggage, stores, and efficient preservation of communica-

* House of Lords, March 3, Contents 125, non-Contents 57. House of Commons, March 21, Ayes 216, Noes 61.

† Vide vol. xi. 7th Edition, chap. li. of "Alison's History of Europe.

tions with the sea coast, probably this armament would amount to not less than twenty thousand men.

There is no foreseeing how suddenly such a contingency might arise, or how secretly a hostile expeditionary force may be again equipped in Europe with the acquisition of Egypt in view. It behoves us therefore to be found prepared at any time to act with *decisive celerity*. It would not be difficult to arrange *beforehand* that an effective force should be *always* available in India to meet with military promptitude *any* critical necessity.

This subject is deserving of the serious attention of the highest authority, as likewise how far desirable it would be to ascertain the number of Sepahees per regiment throughout the native army willing to register themselves *at once* as general service men.

If the number be sufficiently great, general service corps should be immediately organised.

The contingency of foreign service across the seas being at this moment *apparently* remote, less repugnance would be experienced to enter for such corps than when the *actual* exigency arrived.

These views admit of much further discussion.

When a very large force is required for foreign service, a *call* for volunteers is highly impolitic, it might not be met to the extent which the requirements of the occasion imperiously demanded, thereby placing the Government in an embarrassing predicament.

The call for volunteers is at any time a tacit recognition of the soldier's right to exercise a discretionary judgment, as to whether it suited *his* individual views to meet the urgency of the state or not. An unmilitary, and even alarming concession.

Though the call for volunteers, were unresponded to in a proper spirit, yet to meet any such momentous crisis, the Government must *ultimately* be forced peremptorily to direct the embarkation of the required force. Why then *beseech*, when it is to be hoped that the state can *command* without apprehension of defeat.

This view is not applicable of course to a call for volunteers to lead a forlorn hope, (so infelicitously designated by the French as *Enfans Perdus*) or, to a noble band emulous of the glorious risk of self-immolation for the honour and safety of an army.

It is on occasions of foreign service that the moral force of character of the European officer, and his personal influence with the Sepahee, *not the growth of a day's kindly deportment towards the native soldier*, stand the Government in such stead. It is now that the great advantages of a long continued system of a firm, just, and friendly professional intercourse with the Sepahee on the part of his British officer manifest themselves. But this is an important subject reserved for future discussion when the writer comes to speak of the European officers of the native army.

Henceforth, not a man should be entertained but with the *perfect* understanding that he is enlisted for *general service*, and to fight for his salt and the Government which pays, clothes, and protects him wherever the scene of that service may be cast.

Otherwise, this army can be considered in no other light than as a standing militia; and to such Mr. Pitt's bitter sarcasm to a Colonel of Yeomanry would apply with great force and truth. This gentleman, bowing to some compliment paid him by the great minister on the appearance of his corps, observed: "I have one request, however, to make on the part of the corps and myself, which is, that we may not be called upon to serve abroad." "Sir," replied Mr. Pitt, "pray make your mind easy on that score; you will not be called upon to quit the country—except, in case of an *invasion*."

Section the Ninth.

THE BRAHMIN NUISANCE. RESTRICTED RECRUITING. AFRICAN REGIMENTS FOR SERVICE IN INDIA. MILITARY COLONIES. CORPORAL PUNISHMENT.

THE greatest reluctance to serve across the seas is invariably felt, though not openly avowed by the *Brahmin* Sepahees, it is by their secret and jesuitical institutions that the other Hindu classes are encouraged to express repugnance and unwillingness to meet these *just claims* of the service.

For the *military* profession, no such religious interdiction exists, forasmuch, as a Hindu soldier slain in battle, *wherever* that locality may be, is considered to have passed at once into Swurg, or eternal beatitude.

The Brahmin class continues to abound in far greater numbers throughout the ranks of the native army than is generally credited, notwithstanding the positive prohibitions limiting their employ. They now enter as *Chutreeahs* or *Rajpoots*, but invariably in the lines of their respective regiments assume, preserve, and exact with a priestly tenacity their sacerdotal rights and privileges, to the injury of discipline. This influence is at all times pertinaciously inimical to the sturdy and honest discharge of military obligations.

From superstitious fear and reverence, no native officer of inferior class dare complain of a Brahmin Sepahee who has misconducted himself. He shields him in every way from trouble and reproach, connives at his evasion of duty, even permitting other Hindu soldiers of inferior caste to take his tour of sentry for him.

He would be for ever tabooed, and rendered utterly miserable in the lines, were he to institute a complaint against a Brahmin Sepahee. Indeed, what other result can possibly be expected, when by their own religion it is most strictly ordained that to save the life, goods and chattels, fair fame, nay, even feelings of a Brahmin from danger, annoyance, or the breath of scandal, the perpetration of any crime, however enormous, becomes absolved—sanctified—a blessing. For the attainment of such objects, the grossest perjury is viewed as a very innocent device.

It is not to be imagined that Brahmins will report each other for professional dereliction of duty. Every officer of experience must have been struck with the extreme reluctance *invariably* displayed by Hindu soldiers, in giving evidence where Brahmins are concerned or implicated, and that their testimony on such occasions has always to be *wrung* from them by a series of questions in cross examination. Whilst such ethics prevail, it is obvious that this caste is not an eligible one for the British native army. Their own religion scarcely approves of military service as a worldly occupation. They are in every respect an undesirable body from which recruits should be drawn, their early impressions, *odious vices*, petted education for Brahmins, altogether unfit them for the simple and robust habits of soldiers. A crime, the commission of which would brand a Rajpoot with indelible infamy in the estimation of his comrades, might be perpetrated by one of this priestly order with but slight, if any diminution of esteem. To such a degree can bigotry among them blind the judgment. This sect are generally the originators and fomentors of discord and sedition. All military experience proves that the worst character makes the worst soldier, for when severely tried in difficulties and dangers he sinks under them, from the absence of that moral energy and support, which enables the good man to show himself the good soldier in all the arduous and terrible scenes that the changeful aspect of war presents. A wise limit has been *directed* by authority to their employ, and it becomes a very important duty of Commanding Officers of Native regiments to ensure the due enforcement of these instructions, and to see that they are not artfully eluded by this priestly caste entering themselves in too great numbers under false names, and as Rajpoots. This admits of cure by indicting the guilty, and punishing them severely on conviction.

This would eradicate the evil, or very considerably modify it. Should they have enlisted under a false denomination, they would scarcely afterwards presume to assume their sacerdotal character, whereby their power of working evil would be very considerably curtailed. The present close borough system of recruiting in such great numbers from favourite provinces, as Oudh and Behar, is obviously most objectionable, on many and serious grounds. It is desirable that specific instructions were issued on this head, as likewise more full and lucid descriptive returns of caste and province called for; at present they are meagrely defective.

A very great discretionary latitude now obtains in the manner of recruiting, and individual *pre-*

dilections, not always founded on justice or experience, are various and arbitrary, and frequently indulged to the detriment of the best interests of the service.

When any particular caste receives superior and unfair consideration, or greatly predominates in numbers, it may be justly inferred that the regiment wherein this state of things exists is far less under the actual command and control of its British officers, than secretly ruled by the artful chicanery of a native cabal.

The general average of Mahommedans in a native corps is probably about 150, whereas 250 of that useful and intelligent class would approach nearer a just proportion, and, as a rule, tend to the preservation of a more politic equilibrium.

The Mahommedan who has followed rural and agricultural pursuits, makes an excellent and hardy soldier, whereas the inhabitant of towns and cities is proverbially unfit. Of this sect, the Syuds, or lineal descendants of the Prophet, are most intolerant bigots, possess and exercise considerable personal influence over men of their own faith, and, as a class, present serious objections to their entertainment in any numbers.

A considerable fusion of Sikhs, Punjaubee Mahommedans, and Rajpoots, into the ranks of the native army, would unquestionably be attended with *inestimable* benefit. As a common act of justice, the ranks of the native army should be open to every *eligible* * native subject throughout the British eastern empire, instead of being confined, as at present, to particular districts and provinces. Nothing would tend more effectually, rapidly, and safely, to break down *bigotry* and *false pride* of caste in the native army, than this wide-searching yet imperceptible reformation in the system of recruiting still blindly followed. As now constituted, with its operating exclusiveness, the native army presents entirely the appearance of a favourite cliqued militia, chiefly composed of Brahmins and Rajpoots, who again are mostly natives of the same provinces, and all imbued with similar feelings, prejudices, and habits of thought. The villany of one artful and influential malcontent, speciously cloaked under the guise of insulted religion, or attack upon caste, becomes the staple stock of general grievance. This silent

* Men of *low* and *degraded* caste, who from time immemorial have been the pariahs of the land, would never answer as soldiers. Honour and shame are unknown to them. Despised through countless ages, they have never felt the sentiment of self-respect. When no disgrace can humiliate, it is folly to imagine that military glory would be sought at the peril of existence. The introduction of such men into the native army would be equivalent to sealing its death-warrant.

fusion of every eligible class, with the whole length and breadth of our eastern possessions as recruiting ground, besides increasing the moral and physical efficiency of the Indian army, would powerfully assist in subduing that intolerant and baneful *fanaticism* of caste which now retards all real military excellence. It would likewise extend the sphere of British influence by the wider and more *impartial* diffusion of hopes and expectations. The greater and more general the amalgamation of *all respectable* classes into the ranks of the native army, the more efficient and *morally* consolidated will it become. Its tone would gradually improve; and when an army experiences an honourable pride in being identified with all the undertakings of the Government it serves, whether in peace or war, it has become in its character and feelings a patriotic one. A mere mercenary army must at all times hold a far inferior rank in moral estimation, as consisting of men solely influenced by sordid considerations, and therefore only acting from the meanest promptings.

The writer would much like to see a recruiting depôt established at the Cape of Good Hope, and by degrees some 10,000 or 15,000 of the up-country Africans distributed throughout the whole native army. They are a most robust and courageous race, and without any violent sectarian prejudices. Their scruples to cross the seas might be overcome by tact and kindness. They would prove a most valuable acquisition and *counterpoise.* Being foreigners and thus transplanted, they would naturally identify themselves in all things with the British Government. As British subjects, their introduction into the native army would not be viewed as expressive of distrust.* The military amalgamation of distinct races, most unlikely, from their total dissimilarity of feelings and ideas, ever to coalesce for collusive objects, is the basis on which a *mercenary army should ever be constructed.*

When unfit for further active service, they might be located on military farms, where the residue of their lives would be passed in contented ease, and cheerful but not over laborious employment.†

They might prove the nucleus of a very valuable agricultural class.

* The Ghoorka regiments in the British service are composed of subjects of a *foreign state;* and by late instructions from the home Government, their nationality is to be inviolable. There can be no doubt as to the sound wisdom of this policy.

† The principle of military farms for the native army is deserving of the most serious consideration, as one, in its benevolent extension, likely to prove of incalculable benefit to the state.

On this subject much might be advanced to prove its political and military importance both to the Cape colony, and to our eastern empire.

A mercenary army organised upon these principles of amalgamation would possess within itself a far higher impulse of professional emulation, and, by its antagonistic properties, very considerably lessen those reasonable apprehensions which a mere mercenary force *should ever occasion.*

The only security for the continued good conduct of such a body of men is the most religious observance of all engagements on our part, and the rigid exaction of discipline on theirs.

Discipline, as applied to soldiers, is a word of very full and comprehensive signification.

Of late years, with increased emoluments, the discipline of the native army has been relaxed, and the authority of the European officer curtailed. He has little power to reward merit, and still less to punish delinquency.

The theories of well meaning but inexperienced philanthropists have been too readily permitted to exercise a great and pernicious influence in the legislation of military criminal matters.

Though the writer is sincerely assured, that their views are founded on the highest and purest motives, the fear of God and the love of man, yet with equal sincerity he is not the less firmly convinced, *that mistaken philanthropy is grievous severity in the sequel.*

This amiable clamour from without has obscured the judgment of experience.

The total abolition of corporal punishment was found so hurtful in practice, that its limited restoration was provided for in the articles of war for the native troops made in 1845. Every officer of humanity, however much he deplores the necessity, cannot yet resist the conviction of experience, that its existence is indispensable for the proper preservation of military discipline, and must continue in force, so long as uneducated human nature remains unchanged. The reduction of penalties, and almost entire abrogation of corporal punishment have been attended with very injurious results. The Sepahees failed to discern the principles which suppressed its infliction, when they observed the same crimes, formerly thus visited, still occurring in the ranks.

The benevolent theory which dictated the measure was entirely misconstrued by their untutored minds.

It is not the infliction of the lash itself, but the crime which disgraces. The truth of this has been conceded, inasmuch as dismissal from the service does not *now* follow as an inevitable consequence of corporal punishment, nor is it enforced, unless the crime committed has presented features of a debasing character. There have not been wanting instances of soldiers brought to the halberts both in the British service and native army, whose subsequent meritorious conduct has advanced them to the commissioned grade. It is a pleasing and well established fact, that this mode of correction was very sparingly resorted to in the Bengal army, and the writer is happy to add, from the general good behaviour of the men, seldom required, yet there can be no question, but that its wholesome conception much contributed to this salutary moral effect. Since the comparative withdrawal of this corrective influence, crimes of a highly insubordinate complexion, formerly rare in the ranks of the native army, have become of frequent and painful repetition.

Severity is not advocated, but the delegation of proper authority to visit military delinquency in a *suitable* manner. Simple imprisonment is not a desirable punishment for many misdemeanours that soldiers commit. During the term of the offender's confinement, his professional services are lost, the good man in the interim has to perform his duties, and increased duty is imposed for his safe custody; nor is the incarceration any great visitation to an indolent-minded native, who probably views its duration with apathetic, if not even pleased, indifference.

Whereas the infliction of corporal punishment for military transgression would have far better upheld discipline, deterred from the commission of similar offence by the *spectacle* of its prompt and sharp retribution, operated as a warning to the turbulent, returned the culprit the sooner to the performance of his military duties; and if he had submitted to his punishment with a manly firmness, without any diminution of good opinion in the estimation of his comrades: he had committed a breach of discipline and expiated it, and there the matter ended.

The writer has conversed with numerous native officers and intelligent Sepahees on this subject, and their opinions were decided, that corporal punishment could not be abolished without great detriment to the service.

Indeed, its abolition is one of those humane crotchets abundantly shown to be palpably inapplicable to uneducated soldiers. The man of a well regulated mind will by steady prudent conduct avoid the penalty, whilst the brutal and ferocious one *defies*, and *deserves* it.

If the legitimate object of all punishment be to discourage crime, then crime should be *suitably* visited, that this benevolent object be duly attained. Simple discharge from the service for misconduct cannot be viewed as a fit or adequate vindication of outraged discipline.

A soldier may have been professionally educated, clothed, and fed at the public expense for some years, and yet can thus, by the *intentional* commission of an offence, compel his discharge with scathless impunity, at the very time probably that his services are most wanted!

An army to be truly efficient should be governed by *practical professional* knowledge, and not *maudlinised* by philanthropic theories. A large body of uneducated soldiers can only be kept under proper moral and military subjection by the hope of *professional* reward, and the fear of punishment; by fear, is to be understood the dread of incurring the displeasure of authority, with all consequent penalties. This healthy apprehension withdrawn, one of the strongest incentives to continued good action is lost.

It is a recorded saying of Marshal Turenne, one of the most perfect and humane of commanders history has made mention of, that "a good soldier fears his general more than the enemy." Such a feeling is the very foundation of military excellence.

The Sepahee must be raised in his own moral estimation, by implanting a sentiment of honour, and discouraging *delight in hopes of plunder*, and all such unworthy and debasing motives of action. If his military character were formed on such principles, his moral conduct would be uniform and consistent under all circumstances; cowardice and dastardly marauding would be alike hateful in his eyes. The barbarous custom, though less frequent than before, but still occasionally practised, of giving up a conquered town to plunder for a time, is a disgrace to human nature, odious and pernicious in every respect. So long as this barbarism exists, the moral training of troops must be grievously interfered with by the act of the commanders themselves.

The assertion of some writers, that it was this apprehension of the system of corporal punishment, which deterred men of high caste from énlisting in the British service is entirely refuted by the well-known fact that even when the system was in full force, considerable difficulty was always experienced in preventing Brahmins (the highest caste) from entering in too great numbers. Of late years it appears to the writer that every attempt has been made to remove all salutary restraint, and induce the minds of the Sepahees to flow into a *mercantile* channel.

Improve the mind and the *motives of action,* and corporal punishment becomes virtually the mere ghost of the imagination, yet nevertheless a Familiar that whispers occasionally friendly caution to the evil disposed. This impression would not be a *physical,* but a *moral* one, an apprehension of incurring personal disgrace, and it is this feeling alone which can create a generous and military spirit—a firm and uniform conduct.

The writer is assured that the retention of corporal punishment is absolutely politic, requisite, and *merciful.* No one would more sincerely rejoice than himself to see its necessity altogether cease.

But before this can occur with safety to the honour and discipline of armies, the moral tone of the soldier must be cultivated and improved, and his mind educated and exalted.

Section the Tenth.

REGIMENTAL SCHOOLS. NATIVE COURTS MARTIAL. NATIVE COMMISSIONED OFFICERS.

NOTHING would more fully strengthen discipline and improve the moral tone than an impetus given to mental education, for it is invariably remarked, that the Sepahee who can read and write is usually the best conducted, and cleanest in dress and appointments of any man in the company. He has justly risen in self-respect, and is therefore naturally anxious to retain both it and the acquired good opinion of his superiors. He has something *morally* to shield and maintain.

The regimental school in a native regiment, though encouraged by the pecuniary support of Government, receives little or no attention from the European regimental officers. At the present moment, it is in every sense of the word a mere *nominal* institution, from which no real gain is derived. Until these schools are regulated upon some clear and defined system, none of the important and enlightened objects contemplated by

Government can be accomplished. It is questionable whether throughout the whole service five men per regiment attend these schools. It is even doubtful if the *regular* attendance of the teachers is insisted upon in any one corps. They draw the Government allowance, and generally remain idle in the lines—or if they do occasionally afford instruction to the few desirous of receiving it, it is given in their own private dwellings, where they exact extra fees. All this should be put upon a different footing. A monthly roll of those attending the schools ought to be submitted for the information of the commanding officer, distinctly specifying progress, regularity of attendance, and the extent of knowledge acquired by each individual in reading, writing, and accounts.

The school should be visited at least twice a week by interpreters of regiments, and once during the month by the commanding officer. At these visits the proficiency of the men might be ascertained. Without this supervision, and some interest being displayed, no possible advantage can result from its institution.

These detailed monthly reports of the regimental schools might be submitted with advantage for the information of the higher authorities. The character-book of companies ought to specify those Sepahees who attend the school. And the teachers should be called upon to furnish regular reports elucidatory of their labours and results. The great benefits of such a system, perseveringly continued, would declare themselves in a very superior class of native commissioned and non-commissioned officers, springing up in the service, more respected by *themselves*, and by the men, and far better qualified to uphold their own position and advance the real interests of the corps to which they belong.

A proper and friendly concern evinced by the officers of companies in the progress of their men, by occasionally looking in upon the regimental school, would generally assist the objects in view, and create a more general desire for rudimental knowledge.

These visits would afford excellent opportunities of acquiring, from *personal* observation, an acquaintance with the capabilities and disposition of individuals, *correct* information which would prove of much ulterior advantage. The men would be pleased to observe that their characters were judged through *this* medium, and not by ex-parte representations. The happiest results could not but follow the wise and salutary institution of such relations. The personal influence of the British officer would penetrate the whole company, and animate it with a *social* and important spirit. The creation of such a social connexion would strengthen professional ties, and ensure on a solid basis, a uniformity of conduct under *all circumstances.*

At present so few are able to read and write in the ranks of the Native army, *from the absence of proper encouragement,* that great difficulty is always experienced in obtaining properly qualified individuals for the situation of pay-sergeant. Many who hold these important posts are so incompetent as to require, *sub rosâ,* the assistance of more intelligent soldiers to keep their books and accounts. When this occurs, and it is not a singular case, the *unanimity* and discipline of the company are injuriously affected by the influence thus gained by an *irresponsible* individual.

It should be a recognised and strictly enforced principle, never to promote a man beyond the rank of Naick who cannot read and write.

There can be no question if this system of education is firmly and judiciously pursued, that in course of time the Native army will possess a very superior class of Native officers. Those of the present day, with some *rare* exceptions, are notoriously unfit for the commissioned grade, and mentally incapable of performing in an adequate and suitable manner the higher duties required of them.

At present a court martial composed of native officers is a mere absurdity.

They possess none of the qualifications requisite for the proper discharge of their important functions.

They owe their promotion almost solely to seniority, and are entirely without education.

They remain in a state of mesmerism during the whole of the proceedings, and when finally called upon for their opinion, invariably answer the superintending officer with, "Jo, apkee khooshee,*" and can seldom, if ever, be induced to give any other reply.

In truth, the superintending officer is *de facto* both judge and jury; and the fate of the prisoner and the sacred cause of justice, depend entirely upon his individual view of the case—a view that may be right or wrong, according to *his* capacity to form a correct or incorrect judgment. Nor is it unreasonable to apprehend that an officer so situated might be very liable to decide erroneously from a mistaken view of the circumstances.

* "What your honour pleases."

When this happens, the superintending officer ought to decline exercising this serious and gratuitous responsibility, and report for the consideration of superior authority the incompetency of the native members of the court.

The constant repetition of these reports would force upon the attention of the authorities, that the present system of native courts did not operate beneficially, inasmuch, that the accused did not obtain a fair trial; but was solely tried, and condemned, or acquitted, as the case might be, by the fiat of an individual, he the superintending officer of the court, and sometimes, probably, the commanding officer of the prisoner's company.

The writer does not by any means advocate the abrogation of the long-established privilege of the native officers to sit on courts martial; for it might be very mischievously misinterpreted; and indeed would clearly admit of the invidious construction, that by this substitution of European for native officers, greater severity and less chance of escape were contemplated. Besides, it is to be hoped that under the operation of improving causes, the native officers may yet become better qualified to perform those serious and essential duties; at present they are too apt to fashion their tone according to the supposed wishes of their superiors.

The writer would, however, certainly propose that henceforth, until greater eligibility obtains, the *option* of being tried by a native or European court should invariably be *offered* to the accused party. This, of course, entails additional trouble upon the European officers, should the party prefer, as it is more than probable he would, to be tried by British officers; but that ought to be no consideration whatever when so solemn a question as justice is under review.

Of late years the advantages of the native commissioned grade have been very much increased, both in an honorary and pecuniary degree, yet still without success in creating either a proper dignified conception of his position, or of its responsibilities. It is a very painful fact, forced upon attention by numerous circumstances, that this benevolent consideration of Government for the condition of the native officer has failed to animate him to a more zealous and *conscientious* execution of his professional obligations to the state. On all occasions of discontent and insubordinate caballing, how *very rare* is it to see a native officer come forward in a firm and unequivocal manner, to disclose what has come to his knowledge, thereby evincing a becoming consciousness of the duty he owes to his own rank, and to the Government which conferred it. It would be the height of credulity to imagine the possibility of evil intention existing in the lines without his most entire cognition. He, therefore, by failing in moral energy, virtually becomes an accomplice. The manly performance of his duty as a commissioned officer imperatively requires a *prompt* disclosure of such seditious designs.

It is lamentable to know that, with his increased rank, he acquires not the slightest perception of his increased responsibility. He still remains in all his feelings and sentiments a *common soldier*, and seldom assumes the moral tone of a commissioned officer. An apathetic indifference is characteristic of this class. There are some few exceptions to the general rule, and the Sepahees themselves very pointedly draw the line, in their different modes of address. Where the firmer-tempered officer is respectfully approached with "Subadar Sahib," the weak and imbecile one is cavalierly addressed as "Subadar Jee;" the distinction being as between "Sir," and "Thou."

The seniority system, so rigidly adhered to in

the Bengal native army, is glaringly inapplicable to natives, for longevity absolutely becomes the sole *merit*. The exercise of a *greater* discretionary latitude should be *sanctioned* in the selection of men who are to fill such important situations, upon the energetic and *honest* discharge of which, depends in so considerable a degree the efficiency, honour, and safety of the native army.

Otherwise, the native commissioned grade can only be viewed in the light of an *effective superannuated asylum*, which is a solecism in common sense! A few rules might be drawn up, clearly and forcibly defining the nature of the moral duties and responsibilities of native officers, and read and carefully explained once a month to the native officers, in the presence of the whole regiment formed in square. They would thus perfectly understand what was the exact nature of their tenure of office; and the men would distinctly perceive the great risk that the commissioned officer incurred by weakly *shuffling*, when every principle of honour and gratitude required he should act with the most unflinching energy and fidelity. This would give vigour to honest determination, and greatly support authority, by showing the Sepahee that his native officer, in criminally shielding the delinquencies of subordinates, voluntarily courted his own destruction.

Both parties would now be on the *qui vive*, and a proper professional demarcation *felt* and recognised. There can be no doubt but that the regimental schools, regulated on wise and beneficent principles, will produce a far superior class of native officers, and elevate the spirit of the native army. The writer regrets to observe, that this is a subject which has hitherto received scarcely any attention. Experience has abundantly shown that the too liberal bestowal of largesses has awakened other feelings than those of increased fidelity and attachment. *Education*, and the *moral* and *physical* training of soldiers, can alone ensure their continued efficiency and undeviating allegiance. The danger of not recognising these principles, and *applying* them to the native army, may yet be discovered, *when too late.*

Section the Eleventh.

SUPERIORITY OF THE FUSIL TO THE MUSKET. REGIMENTAL GYMNASIA. ADVANTAGES OF A MILITARY POLICE FORCE. DISARMING OF THE POPULATION.

THE Asiatic, as a characteristic of his race—and this is accounted for by the effects of climate and other causes — possesses an inferior volume of muscular development to the European; and yet we overweight the Sepahee with an unwieldy and ponderous musket, which he is unable to handle with *proper* physical efficiency, or to carry with comfort and satisfaction to himself. It is too heavy for the English soldier, strong and powerful as he is in his limbs, more particularly in his arms. And yet, until these weapons are worn out, however much the truth of the above assertion may be recognised, it is more than probable that he will still continue to sweat under the burden of his unwieldy and intolerable *wall piece*.

The fusil, with a somewhat long barrel, fined off towards the muzzle, on the principle adopted in the construction of fowling-pieces, and slightly bell-mouthed, to facilitate the introduction of the cartridge, is clearly the weapon for modern warfare. It would have an equal, if not superior range to the common musket; prove far handier and more efficient; and immeasurably more agreeable to the man who has to use it—no unimportant consideration of itself.

An objection to the fusil is urged by some officers, that it would not be sufficiently weighty in the "charge," or to resist cavalry. Infantry, it is presumed, are not always charging, nor have cavalry any proverbial predilection for approaching squares.

It is not the introduction of a popgun into the army that is advocated, but of a good, strong, and *substantial* fusil, fit for all the purposes of war, very considerably lighter and handier than the present wall piece in use, with the facility obtained of greater freedom of action, and increased advantage to the ends in view.

The object of all military movement being celerity, with precision, the substitution of such a fusil for a ponderous musket *deserves* attention. It would enable the soldier to move with far more ease to himself, and after a hard day's march, or irksome manœuvres in the field before the enemy, there can be no question but that the fire of the fusileer would be sharper and steadier than that of the unhappy possessor of the wall piece. The greatest quantity of fire is but sound; it is only when the ball strikes its mark that reality is produced. That infantry which delivers the quickest and steadiest volume of fire, is the one always most likely to win the stakes.

Under every view, the introduction of this lighter weapon presents superior claims to consideration. It would also be more economical in many respects. Smaller description of pouch—less weight of balled ammunition—in lieu of heavy cross belts, substitution of the single shoulder belt, with sliding frog for bayonet—lighter bayonet and ramrod—cross belts exploded—less wear and tear of uniform by friction; and all these alterations would considerably reduce the weight that the soldier has now *unnecessarily* to stagger and pant under. These changes and improvements would manifestly conduce to the ease and comfort of the soldier's body, add to his cheerfulness and elasticity of spirit, and not a little contribute to his power of enduring the hardships inseparable from a military life.

It is hoped that these suggestions may attract notice in the *right* quarter, as it is sincerely believed that they are deserving of adoption. At least there can be no dispute but what they are entitled to a fair trial before being bigotedly condemned.

If the regimental gymnasium was sanctioned by Government, it could be regulated on a defined system. *It should be a fundamental principle, that no rivalry, no competition of any sort with other corps be allowed.* Those who are well acquainted with the Sepahee character, and know how feuds are engendered and cherished, will easily recognise the *absolute* necessity of this positive prohibition, as a primary and *important* regulation. That the school should *invariably* be permitted to elect its own *head Teacher*, or Oostad, and only this one recognised in the regiment. It will only be by this understood recognition, that chances of party questions will be altogether prevented. It should be the *duty* of the officer of the day to attend, and see that good order and amity are preserved. The natives of India possess such institutions among themselves, and by them the Palæstra is designated Ukhara, in which wrestling, single stick, sword and dagger exercises, wielding of moogdars,* the Lézum,† and raising of the Naul,‡ with various other gymnastics, are taught upon scientific prin-

* Wooden clubs. † Iron chain bow.
‡ Heavy weight of wood or stone.

ciples, under the general appellation of Wurzish, or, the art of gymnastics.

These exercises are admirably adapted to form soldiers for the practice of their profession. They are also obviously well calculated to contribute to the preservation of health, and to the formation of a strong bond of union, as among the members of a family. Under every view, but more essentially as respects the moral and physical training of the Sepahee, the introduction of regimental gymnasia into the native army is a subject deserving of important consideration.

The writer cannot coincide in the views of some distinguished commentators on the native army, that it would be desirable to open out hopes of eventual employment in the police establishment, provided military conduct during effective service had been unexceptionable. The proposition carries an appearance of absurdity on the very face of it. Is the regular army to be considered as the nursery of policemen?

The idea is only one degree less preposterous, than if, inversely, the police establishment held out prospects of transfer to the line; this at all events would cherish a *military* sentiment, whereas the other system unquestionably conduces to the extinction of all professional tone and principles.

It would sap the foundation of military virtue, by encouraging and increasing to a fearful extent the simulation of diseases, and other malingering artifices, practices in which the Sepahee is no mean proficient, whereby to obtain this *otium cum dignitate* of police retreat. It is unreasonable to anticipate, if this establishment became one of desire, that soldiers anxious to enter it would display any very ambitious spirit for distinction, or court any risks that might endanger the chances of realising such unworthy expectations. Surely no one, on calm reflection, can seriously advocate the placing of so derogatory a motive before a man following the profession of a *soldier?* The advantages of the military service are great and manifest, and its invalid provision most generous and liberal. An honest and proper minded soldier should fix all his hopes and ambition upon his profession, and with his breast decorated with the honorary insignia of a veteran, decline coveting the situation of a policeman.

Besides, if a *well organised* military police of horse and foot is ever established in India, as in every way so desirable of accomplishment, it should contain none but *able bodied* and *effective* members. Otherwise no possible benefit can follow its formation. The police force of Great Britain contains as fine a body of men as can be found in the ranks of the regular army. Good conduct, firm, but temperate discharge of duty, with proper wholesome respect for authority, have ever been the distinguishing characteristics of this most respectable body. Their excellent personal behaviour on all occasions forms of itself a moral support to authority.

Such a description of police, formed on military principles, should be *ample* to preserve the good order and tranquility of the *Lower Provinces*. If raised, and only employed as a *local militia*, it would soon become a very popular service. Natives of respectability would be desirous of holding rank in it. They should be well armed and well disciplined; but not clothed in the uniform of the regular army, nor entitled to honorary military distinctions. Exclusively a civil force, with a military education, but all offences tried by civil process. The commandant possessing the powers of a magistrate both in the district, and over his battalion, would relieve the civil officer from those duties which now occupy and remove his attention from more important functions, and which should exclusively employ his time and consideration. The civil authorities of the district ought to possess no right of interference whatever with the military police, nor should it be called upon to furnish personal guards, or be employed in any way out of its proper line of duties. The present Thana police is notoriously corrupt and inefficient, and it can scarcely be otherwise with its almost entire immunity from strict *European* supervision. It feasts on the people, and winks at delinquencies. The higher posts in it are usually bought and sold. Men would gladly enter this *reformed* police on a monthly pay of five rupees, with a graduated scale of promotion, and a small pecuniary increase attached thereto.

Mere seniority should constitute no claims to promotion, which should depend entirely on merit and peculiar fitness.

The men must be enlisted to serve for twenty-one *years* before being entitled to invalid pay. Otherwise the grave consideration presents itself how far politic it would be to train so vast a portion of the population in the disciplined use and knowledge of arms. If entertained between the ages of twenty-one and twenty-five, and on the above stipulations of service, all apprehension on this score would cease; as when returned to the body of the people, the policeman would never be under forty-two years of age, at which period of life, the native of India in point of physical energy is about on a par with the European sexagenarian. The principle being, the writer presumes, to keep up an effective *police* force, and not the gradual formation of a Landwehr in India.

The organization of this military police presents so many advantages that they must strike every one. The regular army will by its institution be relieved of numberless anomalous duties, and thereby kept in an *effective* military state of efficiency. The same may be said of the Irregular Native Cavalry. In course of time a very considerable saving in the military expenditure of the country might be effected with entire safety and good policy.

The most important and beneficial result of the formation of such an *efficient* protective force would be the acquired *right* of peremptorily disarming the *whole population of British India*, making it a very serious misdemeanour to bear arms without legitimate authority. At this moment throughout India, probably every third man is the possessor of warlike weapons of some description or other. This armed state of society fosters a spirit, which is always unfriendly to the wholesome restraints of law and civilization.

The circumstances attending the emeute at Allahabad in 1848, furnish sufficient and positive proof of the impolicy of allowing a population to remain armed—on this occasion some 8 or 10,000 men assembled in arms—lives were lost, constituted authority insulted and defied, various outrages of a most flagrant description perpetrated, and a very dangerous example of lawless violence presented for future imitation. The province of Allahabad alone could turn out 20,000 men in the course of a very few days, to whom the handling of warlike weapons has been familiar from their youth. During the siege of Bhurtpore in 1826, many provinces offered the spectacle of an unauthorised warlike array, and remained during the siege operations in a very unsettled and turbulent state.

In fact, this disloyal unsteadiness during time of war is quite characteristic of India.

The evil and its *only* antidote are very apparent.

The disarming of the population, with the healthy and energetic operation of the military police, could but tend most effectually to ameliorate the condition of society. With increased security afforded to life and property, by the *hunting down* of crime, the public mind would be tranquilized, and the resources of the country still further improved and developed.

The truly grand and noble efforts of the British Government for the suppression of Thuggee,—which have been so eminently successful, encourage the hope that here also there will be no deficiency of a determined and wise philanthropy in eradicating a social mischief of *enormous magnitude.*

With temperate firmness there would be no difficulty in achieving this great victory of civilization over barbarism.

Section the Twelfth.

THE EUROPEEN OFFICERS. REGIMENTAL DUTY UNPOPULAR WITH THEM. PROFESSIONAL AND MORAL TESTS FOR STAFF EMPLOY. ORDER OF MERIT. EXCLUSIVENESS OF EUROPEAN OFFICERS. REGIMENTAL STAFF.

THE European officers of the native army are the links by which its unswerving attachment and discipline are preserved—this chain once weakened—the whole series becomes disturbed and vibrates towards destruction. It is chiefly upon the zeal, loyalty, competency and conciliatory deportment of the European officers that the efficiency and allegiance of the Sepahees must depend. The British officer of the Native army must always look upon himself as a very closely connected part of it. Should he in the smallest degree alienate himself from the men, or in any way evince by his demeanour, that their interests and professional honour are something distinct from his, or superciliously neglect to become acquainted with all the circumstances of those under his command, he is deficient in a most essential portion of his professional qualifications.

Unless he is familiar with all their habits and peculiarities, and properly mindful of their just rights and requirements, it is impossible that he can exercise any personal influence amidst trials and dangers, or prove capable of animating them during the arduous and trying scenes of war. The proud eminence achieved by a lengthened and brilliant military career, consecrated by a host of renowned memories, has established the reputation of the British Sepahee on a glorious foundation, and it only remains with his British officer of the present day, to prove that he is able to lead and command him. The tone of a native regiment is more affected by the personal conduct and disposition of its European officers than is generally imagined. To *a far greater* extent does this influence work for good or evil than in an European corps, wherein a strong spirit of nationality prevails,—with a corrective Christian sense of right and wrong.

When an active transfer from regiments to staff employ is of daily occurrence, it is utterly impossible that the European officer can acquire any knowledge of the character and qualities of Sepahees, or feel a desire to obtain it.

His hopes and ideas are elsewhere—his feelings cannot therefore be interested in the welfare of a body from whom he is so eager to separate—nor is it reasonable to expect that their attachment will be fixed upon an officer who evinces such disinclination to be identified as a friend and protector. It has always been observed that where men and officers have been long associated, rising through the respective grades in progressive advancement, that strong feelings of mutual confidence and attachment have invariably been created. Every military man of experience is well aware, that the good or bad conduct of regiments is mainly dependent upon the presence or absence of such moral incentives.

European officers must be viewed as constituting the moral force of regiments. Especially so, when corps are formed of foreign levies, as those of the native army of India. And if in Europe, the moral is to the physical, as 5 is to 3; in India, it may be considered as 50 to 1.

The effective regimental strength of officers of H. M.'s regiments is 45, that of a regiment of native infantry 23! And yet the latter goes into action, on account of the number of its regimental officers absent on staff employ, with even a still greater disproportion of officers, and suffering consequently under the most serious and vital disadvantages.

It frequently happens, from the number of officers absent on staff employ, that in action there is not a British commander to every company of a regiment of native infantry. Those posts are therefore necessarily occupied by native officers, averaging from sixty to seventy years of age, who find it a physical impossibility to keep up with the line or column. They are scarcely of any use but to stop a bullet.

As operations in the field are generally over very rough and intersected ground, sometimes in deep sand, these brave but superannuated veterans, from sheer exhaustion, are absolutely during a rapid advance left behind. More deeply wounded than if struck down by the shot of the enemy. The fact, that this state of things cannot continue without a manifest tempting of providence, must be apparent to the meanest capacity. The regiments of native infantry are notoriously underofficered.

It is not unusual to point to a local corps, with its three officers (frequently one absent) as disproving the opinion that the efficiency of a native corps of the line depends upon a full proportion of European officers. In the first place, these irregular corps are rarely tried in the same manner as troops of the line; nor would they prove either very efficient, or *effective,* if employed for any lengthened period out of their own immediate districts, or strict sphere of duties.

They could not be brought through the stern ordeal of a well contested *general* engagement, as native regiments are, under the energetic leading of their British officers. Besides, if the commandant should happen to be killed, or placed *hors de combat,* the confidence of an irregular corps would be greatly shaken, if not destroyed. The second in command, generally viewing his situation as a sinecure, knows little of the men, and they less of him. *Under these circumstances,* he would not at a critical moment supply the place of the commandant, with that *moral* efficiency which could alone give every hope of success. The adjutant is usually a young officer of some three or four years standing. He who cannot be reasonably supposed to possess much influence or experience.

The institution therefore of a comparison between regiments thus disproportionately officered, and to conceive that a local corps could vie in real efficiency with a regiment of the line, would appear a mere *façon de parler.*

The European subaltern officer of the native army too generally looks upon the performance of regimental duties as a task, irksome, if not humiliating. He has little ambition to acquire the character of a good regimental officer. He has scarcely joined the corps, when every effort is strained to quit it, so as to escape from what he is apt to pronounce drudgery and thraldom.

Did he endeavour by an assiduous cultivation of professional knowledge, of the native languages, habits, customs, and prejudices, to qualify himself for the employ he seeks on the general staff of the army, *then* his aspirations would be meritorious, and highly deserving of reward.

But in too many instances he grounds his hopes solely on the adventitious possession of personal or family interest. Such expectations, founded on private considerations, are however frequently realised. He who won the sea-fight of Salamis has left a saying: that it was his rule to serve his friends first, and merit afterwards. A principle which flourishes very luxuriantly throughout the world, and is probably not more the rule in India than elsewhere. Superior ability and industry have as good, if not better chance of reward in India than in Europe, for the machinery of Government in this country would be soon disturbed if important posts were filled without reference to merit and competency. The official intrusion of ignorant apathy would create a complete stagnation if not utter confusion in public affairs.

It cannot be disguised,—that an idea prevails in the service, that merit unsupported by interest is unlikely to succeed. Though there are many and distinguished examples contradictory of this supposition, still facts themselves are of no avail with minds obstinately opposed to conviction.

The only remedy would appear to be the institution of strict professional tests, whereby the peculiar eligibility of individuals for employ in any particular branch of the public service could be fully elicited. The candidate should previously declare what line of the service he was desirous of entering, and the test of examination applied accordingly. The whole talent of the services ought to be available for these important duties, and to ensure their execution with becoming strictness and impartiality, the members should be duly sworn. This would obviate all scruples of delicacy on the part of the examiners, and point out to the aspirant the necessity of coming well prepared. Each candidate should appear before the committee with an analysis of his ideas upon that branch of the service he is desirous to enter. These *brochures*, besides proving of essential public benefit, would tend to elevate the mental tone of the service by animating the dormant energies of its members.

Even should the candidate undergo successfully an examination in these tests of a purely professional nature, he must likewise be able to stand the test of *temper* and of *moral conduct* or *character* before his perfect eligibility was considered fairly established. This plan would effectually subdue all feelings of distrust or *legitimate* professional irritation.

And it is not by any means improbable that those who are now the most clamorous in complaint might on examination be found the least deserving of advancement?

There is no present necessity for entering into a fuller detail of a plan so well adapted as this is to fill the staff situations of the army with properly qualified incumbents, or better calculated, to call forth all the latent zeal and talent of the service. If its utility, importance, and practicability are acknowledged, there is no difficulty in devising a regular system for its realization. The plan of *staff corps* in the native army is a simple impossibility.

A truly great man holding exalted trust in the service of his country should sincerely rejoice at any eligible scheme, which whilst it secured with just impartiality the best talent and most conspicuous merit for the public service, relieved him from irksome and indelicate importunities, with their unpleasant and perplexing train of circumstances.

His emancipation from this thraldom of patronage would in truth be a dignified release from exigent importunity. For, even were it dispensed with the most religious disregard of private feeling—bestowed with the most scrupulous justice, still the balance can never be struck in such a manner as to disarm criticism, or prevent discontent.

By the operation of this plan of professional and *moral* tests, so much would depend upon *real* efficiency, that those desirous of advancing themselves in the service could not but perceive the absolute necessity of acquiring the requisite qualifications.

The existing craving for staff employ has become such an unreflecting passion in the native army as to weaken every sense of *regimental obligations.*

At present, so general is the apathy and indifference with which regimental duties are performed, that the subject has become one of grave consideration. The advantage of instituting an order of merit for the European officers of the army appears to the writer manifest. If conferred on real desert, it would be regarded as an honourable distinction, and as a proof of professional excellence, would stimulate the best energies of the whole army for its acquisition. Regimental duty is now too much *got through* in a lifeless mechanical manner. The institution of this order would be well calculated to raise the tone of the army; for to a soldier *pecuniary* reward should be altogether subordinate to the desire of professional military distinction. There is no question but what this army contains numerous officers who regard honours and distinctions as far superior to considerations of *purse*. It is a most unquestionable defect in the constitution of an army, when the spirit of men of this stamp cannot be gratified. All officers have not opportunities of distinguishing themselves in the field, and thereby acquiring brevet rank and honorary decorations.

Circumstances and connexions often afford peculiar advantages to individuals of acquiring notice, and ingratiating themselves with the superior authorities, which their less fortunate but equally deserving brother officers fail to obtain.

A military "order of merit" for the whole army would act as a powerful stimulus to professional exertion, tend vastly to improve regimental efficiency, and allay this irritation caused by observing an officer elevated by brevet rank for services in the field, which his fellow soldiers would have been equally ready and proud to perform, had similar opportunities been afforded them.

In these days, officers of the native army know but little personally of their men, still less of what is going on around them in the lines of their respective regiments. That bond of union founded on reciprocal regard and esteem, and which marked in former times the almost clanlike intercourse subsisting between the Sepahee and his British officer, now scarcely exists. A wide chasm separates the European officer from his native comrade, a gulf in which the dearest interests of this army may be entombed, unless a radical change of relations between the parties is introduced. How often has the truth been reiterated, that the lives of soldiers are commanded through the medium of their affections. The acquisition of this honourable personal ascendancy is a sacred obligation that the young officers of the native army owe to their country, the service, and themselves. They should studiously labour to obtain it, for upon its possession will essentially depend their own professional character and future prospects in the service.

With Sepahees, especially, confidence is yielded only after a long and full appreciation of their British officers, and is invariably with them a plant of slow growth, requiring unceasing kindness and attention to secure its healthy maturity.

A mere cold, dry, and mechanical performance of the routine of duties does not form the Sepahee officer. He must neglect no opportunity of making himself personally known to, and of becoming intimately acquainted with the characters and dispositions of those under him. It is a lesson not learnt in after life. There can be no real good will in the breast of a soldier towards an officer who evinces a callous indifference to his feelings and wants, and only attempts to institute friendly relations when in the field before the enemy.

A previous systematic neglect of them will now render such attempts altogether fruitless. And yet this important influence can be obtained without surrendering one particle of the great principle of military respect and obedience.

Estrangement, proceeding from whatever cause, must inevitably produce injurious consequences to both parties. The recent terrible example of the danger of exclusiveness on the part of the European officer has shown itself in the ruin and disbandment of a whole regiment, under circumstances that should awaken reflection even in the most listless mind. Here were secret meetings and evil communings all confined within a narrow compass, yet those whose duty it was to have been the first acquainted with such dangerous machinations, only received their warning by the explosion of the mine itself. It would be an insult to the meanest understanding to imagine for an instant that the existence of this discontented spirit was hid from the humblest scullion of the camp.

This truly unfortunate event, so simple of prevention, ought never to have occurred. It is only thus briefly touched upon, to observe, that the whole circumstances of the affair disclose how imperatively requisite it is for the European officers to mingle with and know the men as also to make *themselves* known by officer-like acts of kindness and constant solicitude. The secret facility with which things on this lamentable occasion came to a crisis affords another proof of the absence of that happy cordiality and confidence which in recent years has so strongly marked the demeanour of British officers towards the Sepahees. Attention has been called to this subject in a late most excellent general order. Every young officer mindful of his obligations and alive to his own interests, would do well to provide himself with a copy of this order, and *study its principles.* It is the unquestionable duty of an officer in charge of a company to know every individual in it—to be perfectly acquainted with his character, temper, peculiarities, qualifications as a soldier, and the general reputation he bears in the company. This knowledge must be gained by *personal* observation, and not blindly accepted from the lips of a pay havildar, or of any other, perhaps, interested or malicious informant.

The regimental officer should be easy of access and *patient of hearing*—delegate his authority to no one; listen to and redress all grievances himself, and refuse attention to complaints without the presence of the accused party. A good and deserving soldier, be he of whatever caste he may, is equally entitled to the just and impartial consideration of his British officer, who should scorn the weakness of being biassed by native ideas and prejudices, in considering the claims of a soldier, though of inferior caste. The officer known to possess a judgment warped by such insidious counsels and whisperings will never exercise proper moral influence over the minds of his men.

Young officers are disposed to institute false and injudicious comparisons between the European soldier and his native auxiliary. These have received from nature and education, far different physical and moral organizations—their feelings, habits, and ways of thinking are those of different races—and it is fortunate for the stability of this eastern empire that it is so.

The daring and aggressive courage of the European soldier has always been most ably seconded by the brave and devoted gallantry of his native comrade.

The European soldier *himself* appreciates "*Jack Sepahee.*" The *incapacity* of that officer for command, who attempts to undervalue his well-earned reputation, is sufficiently disclosed. Singular to say, when disparaged, it is usually by inexperienced commentators of his own service, who in all probability have never had the good fortune to lead him in the field, or to have acquired any insight into his many good qualities.

These idle and wide-sweeping aspersions are merely demonstrative of " Young England," and juvenile presumption, and which time and better opportunities of forming a correct opinion, will, it is sincerely to be hoped, entirely overcome. An acquaintance with the political and military history of India, would remove these hallucinations. This is a knowledge essentially requisite to the British officer of the native army. For *he* is most supremely ignorant who remains uninformed upon those subjects which more *especially* concern himself.

It must be admitted as a truth, and it is well established by experience, that the officer who in quarters has studied the characters of his men, and evinced a constant and unaffected interest in their welfare, is the commander who will exercise the fullest power over them in the field. The officer who expects a more than *mechanical* obedience from the soldier, after having invariably treated him as a dull machine, betrays a very imperfect acquaintance with the secret springs of the human heart. Heroic and permanent vigour of action can alone be elicited by the firm attachment of soldiers towards their commanders, grounded on mutual assurance of each others' good qualities. The apathetic officer does not inspire this sentiment, nor has he any right to anticipate its manifestation towards himself.

There is a very marked distinction between securing attachment and respect by a firm and considerate exaction of all duties, with the proper repression of every unsoldier-like act, and the courting of popularity, by winking at their neglect, and permitting the commission of marauding acts on the unoffending people of the country.

Nothing is more esteemed or better appreciated by Sepahees, than a rigid and wise impartiality—a virtue in which, from their defective moral education, they are themselves most deficient. It is not difficult to admire a qualification in others, which we are quite conscious of not possessing ourselves, and probably, on that very score estimate more highly.

All officers of experience of the Sepahee character, are well aware how sensible he is of attention and neglect, how susceptible of praise, and by kind and skilful treatment how easily managed. A judicious and friendly intercourse with those in an inferior class of life can easily be established and maintained without the slightest diminution of prestige or personal dignity. Inferiors find no difficulty in distinguishing between an unaffected and consistent kindliness of deportment, and a supercilious condescension or unbecoming familiarity.

That the Sepahees are quite capable of a lasting and ardent feeling of attachment towards those officers who, whilst with the regiment, took a kind and just interest in their welfare, is strongly and very pleasingly exemplified by their always coming to pay a tribute of gratitude and respect to them, whenever casual circumstances bring the parties into each other's neighbourhood after long years of separation.

These interesting meetings, alike so highly honourable to both officer and soldier, must have been witnessed by many.

Those to whom this homage of the heart was paid, were in every sense of the word *Sepahee officers*—men of note and distinction in the profession.

At the present moment, the Sepahees naively ask if the "Sahib logue who now come to India are of different caste to those of former days?" The question is an unpleasing commentary upon the altered demeanour they perceive exhibited towards them by the new-comers.

Young officers are often prone to denominate, and contemn Sepahees as "black fellows." Unless this fatal error is early rectified, such young officers never succeed; they become intensely unpopular, whereby their value to the service is *worse* than nothing, inasmuch as their presence is irritating to the feelings of the men, and hurtful to the public weal. Asiatics are most implacable in their resentments, and rarely forget or forgive injuries and slights.

And yet, with the exercise of a little zeal and urbanity, this failing may be avoided. The character, temper, and peculiarities of British officers are minutely known, and discussed in the lines of their respective regiments.

It is astonishing the accuracy with which the Sepahees judge of the dispositions of their European officers.

Nothing more offends the *amour propre* of the native soldier than neglecting to return his salute; an omission on his part which subjects him to punishment; and yet how constantly is his self-esteem wounded by this act on the part of some officers. If an oversight, the sooner corrected the better; but if proceeding from intentional and contemptuous neglect, it is unofficer-like and plebeian.

The regimental staff appointments, which in former times were becoming objects of ambition to the subaltern officers, are now scarcely considered worth striving for. The consequence is, that they are not always held by the smartest and most competent, for these are bent on getting away from their regiments as quickly as possible, apprehensive that the tenure of these situations might interfere with their obtaining employment on the general staff of the army. The obvious result must be, and is, that regimental efficiency suffers. Good disposition and steadiness, though respectable qualities in themselves, cannot compensate for the loss of superior energy and qualifications. When this state of affairs obtains, the whole tone of a regiment becomes infected and deteriorated by the lethargy and inefficiency of its staff. These honourable appointments have absolutely come to be considered as the refuge of the destitute.

The merits and qualifications of the officers holding these regimental appointments ought to be well known to the proper authorities, and selections frequently made from "*the most worthy,*" (totally irrespective of any claims of interest) for employment on the general staff. Instances of such patriotic disinterestedness would give life and animation to professional exertion. The reasons of such selections might with advantage to the service be promulgated in general orders.

The moral stimulus given by this just discrimination would ameliorate the present Bœotian state of things, and excite a generous spirit of emulation.

But this consideration can only be *justly* exercised, when merit and qualifications declare themselves. Individuals, in appraising their own value, are occasionally forgetful of the rightful claims of the Government upon the energy and conscientious industry of its servants, *in whatever rank they may be placed.*

The fact, that whilst genius and talent too often languish in mournful penury and obscurity in Europe, mediocrity is receiving munificent recompense in India, does not appear to offer itself sufficiently for contented and *abashed* reflection. It is an unfortunate truth every day more glaringly manifesting itself, that the younger officers of the native army are becoming more and more estranged from salutary professional comradeship with their men. An engaging military frankness, with perfect accessibility of approach, and a certain *bonhomie* of disposition have always characterised popular commanders. No men estimate these qualities better than Sepahees.

Section the Twelfth.

THE DUKE'S APPRENTICESHIP IN WAR. MORAL DUTIES OF COMMANDING OFFICERS. REGIMENTAL MESSES. EXAMINATION IN NATIVE LANGUAGES. POSTSCRIPT.

IT is a legitimate pride to bear in mind that "the foremost man of all this world" acquired his first perceptions of the great art of war in the East. It is very reasonable to believe that had it not been his fortune in early military life to serve with the Indian army, in all human probability the world would never have heard of a "Duke of Wellington."

When the great Captain of the age first appeared on the theatre of his European glory, Napoleon observed, "What! they now produce their *Sepahee* general!"* History has replied to the sarcasm! There can be no question *but*

* And France, the "beloved France" of this very Napoleon, has of late formed her own most able officers in her Colonial army. Behold her *African* Generals, Cavaignac, Lamoriciere—and many a gallant comrade besides.

that the germs of the Duke's reputation were fostered by his apprenticeship to the art of war in the East, where extraordinary exactions are ever made on the Leaders of armies. The very peculiar combination of circumstances attendant upon an extensive scale of operations in the East, generally embracing an union of civil, military, and political powers in the office of the commander, demand master spirits, who alone are capable of conducting to a glorious and triumphant issue great undertakings.

It had previously been very much the fashion of British commanders to trust the fate of battles to the mere fire of musketry, but the Duke's superior experience determined the value of skilful tactical arrangement, and that after the general had done *his* duty, the hardihood and courage of British soldiers were always best displayed at close quarters with their enemy.

This experience was gained in India. There commanders are forced to act upon the Spartan maxim, of contenting themselves with ascertaining the *whereabouts* of the foe, without much regarding his numerical superiority.

Confidence in himself and in his troops, enabled the Duke to apply these tactics with brilliant success, in Europe.

The battle of Assye was fought on these principles, and proved that genius in a commander, aided by the valour of the troops, is always crowned with victory.

The extreme gallantry and devotion of the Sepahees were eminently conspicuous on this eventful day, from which History dates the patent of nobility of the "Hero of a hundred fights." This fact stands forward in a prominent point of view. The achievements and devotion of the Indian army have not yet found an Historian worthy of the subject.

The honours and distinctions so tardily and grudgingly bestowed on its illustrious services, have been solely conferred by the *justice* of the *people* of England. Little gratitude does it owe to those whom it has assisted to place on Fame's highest pinnacle.

In the dispatch of the battle of Assye the following paragraphs occur: "I cannot write in too strong terms of the troops; they advanced in the best order, and with the greatest steadiness, under a most destructive fire, against a body of infantry far superior in number, who appeared determined to contend with them to the last, and were driven from their guns only by the bayonet; and notwithstanding the numbers of the enemy's cavalry, and the repeated demonstrations they made of an intention to charge, they were kept at a distance by our infantry."

"The officers commanding brigades, nearly all those of the staff, and the mounted officers of the infantry had their horses shot under them."

The following was the loss of the native troops on this memorable occasion :

	Subdrs.	Jemdrs.	Havdrs.	Trumprs.	R. & F.
Killed	5	13	13	0	228
Wounded...	12	6	39	6	1,138

Those eminent military commanders whose exploits have ennobled the historical annals of their country have been always distinguished by an intimate acquaintance with the details and requirements of their profession. An indifferent regimental officer is unlikely ever to prove a good general of division.

The reputation of this army, and the future efficiency and honour of the younger officers, must be provided for by a firm and judicious exaction of the regulations of the service, as clearly defined, and laid down for their professional conduct and training. A commanding officer who takes no interest in this subject is unfit for his post. He should feel a sincere desire to give a right bent to the minds of his young officers, who in after life will bless their fortune in having been subjected to such early and wholesome supervision.

The happiness and prosperity of their after career in the service will amply reward this honourable and conscientious discharge of duty, on the part of a commanding officer, who whilst contemplating their advancement to eminence and distinction, may justly feel how much his own efforts and advice had contributed to this professional success. A most gratifying reflection to a retired veteran. Unless a commanding officer acts on these principles, he is the greatest enemy that young officers could have had the misfortune to meet. Some commanding officers imagine that their whole duty consists in drilling a regiment by frequent and *lengthy* parades. This is a grievous error. If every object of a morning's parade for exercise cannot be accomplished in an hour, at the furthest, the commanding officer may depend upon it that no good will follow by prolonging it till the attention and temper of those under him are withdrawn and soured. However mortifying it may be to arrive at such a conclusion, he may fairly attribute the fault to himself.

A few movements performed with precision and celerity are of more service to the tone and discipline of a regiment, than half the book of evolutions drawled through with tedious imbecility. Every officer in rotation should be called upon to exercise the battalion under the commanding officer's superintendence; who will find that his officers are as ready to learn as he can be to instruct, provided instruction is afforded in a proper professional spirit, and with *urbanity*. The subaltern officers should be required to make out all the public papers of their companies in their own hand writing for at least two years after receiving charge of a company. This would necessarily bring them into daily intercourse with the men; improve their knowledge of the language; enable them to acquire the respect and attachment of the native soldiers; and perfect them in many other very essential points of duty. Most extensive benefits would follow the strict enforcement of this important and equitable regulation.

It is equitable both to the men, and to the officers; whose bounden duty it is to watch and preside over the just rights and interests of the soldiers entrusted to their charge. It is almost unnecessary to observe that they are paid for the performance of these obligations, as it is conceived, that a higher sentiment will always dictate their zealous and honourable execution.

In every corps in which a mess exists, it should certainly be obligatory on officers to join it. It is one of the social elements of good order and discipline, supported by the pecuniary aid of Government, and if conducted on *correct principles*, an institution admirably calculated to promote and confirm good habits, improve friendly relations between officers, and cherish an honourable feeling of *esprit-de-corps*. Commanding officers should uphold it by their presence, nor is there any reasonable apprehension of their losing in military authority or respect by cultivating a frank and kindly intercourse with their officers. It ought to be a positive rule, that all mess bills are duly adjusted *monthly*, and a certificate to this effect attached to muster rolls, without which the Government mess allowance should be withheld. A regimental mess regulated on these principles would greatly inculcate habits of *just* economy, and foster a manly desire of independence; without which there can be no true ease of mind or respectability. Idleness and debt are the two great stumbling-blocks of the younger European officers of the native army. When the writer first entered the service, the subalterns of the army were contented to mount themselves on the strong serviceable ponies of the country; now-a-days only expensive Arab horses, averaging from 800 to 1,200 rupees, will serve their turn.

To purchase these, recourse must generally be had to the banks. One loan follows another, and the unfortunate borrower becomes irretrievably involved. The whole of his after career,—"Is bound in shallows and in miseries!"

It is not an exaggerated calculation which makes the greater portion of the European officers of the native army labouring under pecuniary embarrassments. Moral prostration inevitably characterises such unfortunate enslavement. These difficulties can only be attributed with some rare exceptions to morbid vanity and culpable extravagance. It is not an unusual spectacle to observe subaltern officers of this army, without any means beyond their pay, the possessors of racing studs!

As the Government possesses the power of making selections for staff employ, it might with great justice and public advantage, interpose its privilege of ascertaining the pecuniary liabilities of officers before confirming appointments. Conferring or withholding these posts, according to the nature and magnitude of those entanglements, and their apparent disqualifying circumstances.

There can be little doubt that this strong discountenance of debt and its train of evils in such a quarter, would effectually work a decided and a *permanent* cure.

It appears to the writer that the members of committees of examination in the native languages should be *sworn,* as is customary with the members of courts martial. At present it is notorious that while occasionally the examination is unnecessarily severe and arbitrary, too generally it is defectively lenient. The members being henceforth sworn, and the tests furnished by the examiners of the College of Fort William, would place all candidates on an equal and impartial footing. This system would ensure the satisfactory attainment of the legitimate objects of Government, and render the examination literally what it ought to be, but at present is not.

There is every reason why adjutants and medical officers should undergo a precisely similar examination as that required of Interpreters, before being considered eligible for important situations with *native* regiments.

The absolute justice of this rule is so apparent as to require no further advocacy for its adoption. On a new organization of the army, consequent to the establishment of an effective military police force, (which will secure the permanent effective efficiency of regiments of the line,) it would be *highly desirable* that battalions were reduced to *eight hundred* men. An unwieldy corps of one thousand men cannot be exercised with advantage, from the physical impossibility of giving the word of command in such an effective intonation of voice, as to ensure its being distinctly heard by every soldier of the regiment. This is a recognised principle acted upon in all the armies of Europe, and obviously only departed from in battalions of native infantry on account of their effective strength being always so much reduced by the *numerous anomalous duties, escorts, and commands required of them.*

This reduction, besides proving a positive advantage to the efficient manœuvring of troops, will effect a very *considerable and practical saving.*

This is an important and truly desirable object

of attainment. For it is a well known fact, that the present enormous military expenditure of India is every year seriously increasing the financial embarrassments of the local Government.

National honour, and the true interests of the Indian army are inseparably involved in the wise policy of introducing *every* measure of a firm economy, whereby all *reasonable* anxiety as to the future may be allayed, and the integrity of present engagements and stipulations of service preserved on an *unfluctuating* basis.

These remarks are now concluded: perhaps to some they may seem too lengthy—to others several of the extracts quoted and of the points discussed, may be already familiar. The writer would fain think that such must be the case; and he wishes he could persuade himself that an acquaintance with the history and with the character of the native army were more common. It is in the belief that the European officers of the army are not generally so well versed in this essential knowledge of their service and of their men that he has put forth these Musings. His quotations from other writers he believes highly necessary to be known by every officer of whatever standing: and where the author has set forth his own views, he has done so in the consciousness that they are the honest unbiassed convictions of many years experience: and in the hope that they may induce others to think as deeply on the interests and minutiæ of their honourable profession as he has endeavoured to do himself.

Supplementary Chapter.

STERN RETRIBUTION WITH WISE DISCRIMINATION. UNREFLECTING BLOODTHIRSTINESS REPRESSED. FINAL EXIT OF THE LAST OF THE MOGHULS ON THE HIGHEST PINNACLE OF THE KOOTUB MINAR. DELHI, ITS SUBSEQUENT TREATMENT. COMMANDED BY FORTIFIED WORKS. RE-PEOPLED. INDIA CAN ONLY BE HELD BY THE SYMPATHY OF THE POPULATION WITH BRITISH RULE.

After an interval of seven years, events have fully justified and confirmed the preceding remarks on the state and discipline of the Bengal army. Without laying claim to any extraordinary amount of foresight, the author may surely be pardoned if he presumes to draw public attention to the fulfilment of his predictions. Would, indeed, that he had proved a false prophet! But, writing as he did with an intimate knowledge of the subject, it is not surprising that he was able to lay his finger on the first indications of disease, and foretel the certain consequences of neglect.

Balancing the good and bad points of the

native soldiery, he was induced to advocate the necessity for a gradual and judicious reform. The passive but impulsive temperament of the Sepahee suggested the expediency of keeping him fully employed, and thus withdrawing him from the evil promptings of idleness. The author further commented on the thoughtless encouragement afforded by many European officers to the unmilitary prejudices of their soldiers; and he also condemned the reserved and exclusive habits which were perceptibly gaining ground. The generality of officers took but little interest in their men, who, on their part, ceased to feel either love or reverence for superiors who were virtually strangers to them, and powerless, besides, either to reward or punish.

The heroism formerly displayed by Sepahees in the deadly breach and on many a well-fought field could hardly now be looked for, in the author's opinion, from men who had come to regard their profession as only a means of hoarding pelf. The time had been, indeed, when neither threats nor promises could shake their fidelity; but what reliance can be placed on those who are ever ready to mutiny whenever a modification of their allowances is proposed! The copious infiltration of the Brahmin element he denounced as an evil of alarming dimensions; and, by way of counterpoise, recommended the introduction of 10,000 to 15,000 Africans, and a like number of Sikhs and Punjabees, together with a proportionate reduction of the regular troops; a suggestion which others have revived and repeated during the last few months. The mistaken philanthropy of the age was duly censured, and the necessity and advantages of corporal punishment clearly pointed out. The inefficiency, or rather the utter uselessness, of the native commissioned officers was demonstrated beyond a doubt, and the folly of regarding senility as meritorious placed in a proper light.

The want of sympathy between the European officers and their men appeared to the author as fraught with impending peril, and there could be no doubt of its impairing the efficiency of any regiment. He deeply regretted the unprofessional eagerness manifested by officers of all ranks to get away from their regimental duties: nor did he regard with less apprehension the paucity of officers doing duty with each native corps.

It is with no feelings of elation, or self-complacency that the author looks back upon the recent corroboration of all his statements, and the fulfilment of his warnings. But, from a sincere belief that the subject cannot be too fully investigated, he has been induced to place a second time, and in a more prominent manner, before a British public the result of his own experience during a long period of military service. Whatever may be the imperfections of his style, he ventures to entertain a hope that the opinions of an old soldier will not be altogether devoid of interest in the present position of our Indian Empire.

It cannot be denied that the recent revolt of the Bengal army has displayed, in a remarkable degree, the sterling qualities of the Anglo-Saxon character. The invincible fortitude of our countrymen, their heroic self-devotion, their unshaken confidence in the ultimate triumph of the cause for which they fought, and bled, and yielded up life itself, have added fresh lustre to the British name. The verdict of the present age, and one which history will assuredly ratify, unhesitatingly recognises the constancy with which this true and manly spirit has shone forth in all the horrid scenes of this fearful Indian tragedy.

The numerous graphic and touching letters, and narratives, which have become familiar to the entire civilized world, afford an irrefragable testimony to the bravery and worth of our sorely tried countrymen. There have been no manifestations of a quailing heart, no weak expressions of despondency, no despairing and selfish lamentations, in the midst of unspeakable horrors, such as few before have ever encountered and survived. Far from it. While life remained, one and all, they have stood unflinchingly at their posts. There is not a single instance of the postponement of public to private duty—not one, of the natural desire of self-preservation superseding the obligations due to their profession and their country.

No family interest has once been exerted to enable the holiday warrior to escape, on the plea of "leave of absence," or of "urgent private affairs," from the dangers and privations inseparably connected with the noble and chivalrous profession of arms.

Justice and truth demand this poor and inadequate tribute to the heroism of those undaunted Englishmen—aye, and English women, too—who have never faltered in the hour of unutterable woe, in doing their duty to their God and their country. Their calm fortitude under the most appalling sufferings, their valour in fight, their Christian patience under excruciating tortures, their resolute and steadfast spirit, cannot fail to awaken sentiments of the highest respect, admiration, and sympathy in the most cold and callous mind.

And their trials have come upon them suddenly and unexpectedly, under a tropical sky, and in the hottest and most fatal season of the year, while destitute of the commonest comforts and appliances of civilized life.

In all these dismal scenes of anguish, the national character has been nobly upheld by all her children, without distinction of sex. And this is a glorious consolation, which time itself can never lessen nor obscure. Without instituting the invidious comparison with the people of any other country, it may be safely averred, that such daring enterprise, such marvellous endurance, such true greatness of mind, are unparalleled in the world's history.

It is not requisite to enter into any elaborate refutation of the erroneous opinions of some writers, that the European officers of the Bengal army were entirely unacquainted with the changed spirit of the Sepahees. Proof to the contrary is on official record. Journals and publications of deserved reputation and weight have likewise inculcated the idea, that the officers had fallen asleep on a mine, unconscious of its existence. It is not so: many officers of experience and mature ability have, doubtless, considered it their duty to submit their views on the obvious necessity of change and reform in the constitution of the native army of India. This would be but in character with the zeal and devotion of officers whose good services are not unknown or forgotten. But it is not the wish of the writer at present to dwell upon the able, heroic bearing of our Indian officers. In their efforts to maintain their lofty position in the dismal and deadly strife now convulsing our eastern empire, they *have* the sympathy of all true Englishmen.

The writer would, however, direct attention to the unpatriotic few, now busy in filching from the hard-earned reputation of those whose blood has flowed like water, in maintaining the honour and interests of their country. Those who industriously institute such miserable comparisons, will perhaps favour the public with some account of themselves, and disclose how *they* have met the temptations, and buffeted the stern realities of life? The writer, in 1849, now more than eight years, deferentially submitted his opinions on the manifest advantages of incorporating Sikhs and Punjabees with the Bengal Regular Army. And having raised the first Sikh regiment ever employed in the British service, and led it with success against its own countrymen and co-religionists, he was surely entitled to hope that his opinions on such a subject were not altogether undeserving of some respect and consideration.

This *brochure* was presented by the writer to the Governor General, who approved of its contents, and placed it in the hands of the late General Sir Charles Napier, then Commander of the Forces in India. He read it, and informed the writer that after making many marginal notes he had returned the *brochure* to the Governor General; he further expressed his entire concurrence with the views therein advanced. It is a great satisfaction to have possessed the friendship and good opinion of that truly British and illustrious Commander, by whom the writer was selected to organise the Punjab Irregular Force for service on the Derajat frontier.

In 1850, the writer published opinions bearing on the Constitution of the Native Army, and suggested various, and, in his humble judgment, most requisite changes. These views in the form of a pamphlet were by permission dedicated to the Governor General. In the same year, he submitted the memorandum marked A in Appendix.

Again, in 1852, he solicited attention to the same subject, *vide* Demi-Official Letter, marked B.

On assuming command of the troops that were to compose the Punjab Irregular Force, he, with the sanction of Government, introduced 200 Sikhs and Punjabees into each infantry regiment, and 150 into each corps of cavalry. This force has remained faithful in spite of the defection of the regular army. Several regiments have been employed in the late operations before Delhi, and distinguished themselves in its final assault and capture. The plan is unfolded in the opinions herein set forth.

To disenchant a powerful body of mercenaries of the idea that they were irresistible, and could at any moment overthrow the Government, and rival the Janissaries of old in unbridled license and domination.

To establish a System of Military Labour. The introduction of a vast accession of new levies of entirely antagonistic elements into the ranks of the regular native army.

To reduce the Hindoostanees to the extent of 200 men per regiment.

The operation of these arrangements in the Bengal line alone would, in their moral and physical effect, have been equivalent to a change of 50,000 men. The advantages of these measures of reform must strike the most superficial reader.

The author further pointed out, that "of late years, with increased emoluments, the discipline of the native army has been relaxed, and the authority of the European officer curtailed. He has little power to reward, and still less to punish delinquency." He also observed that "the worst character makes the worst soldier," and earnestly solicited attention to the serious importance of improving the motives of action of a vast standing mercenary army. These suggestions are also applicable to the armies of Madras and Bombay. We must make our mercenaries *feel* and *understand* that they are more in need of us than we of them. Above all things, the discipline of troops should be left with their proper officers.

The improper, highly dangerous, and irresponsible interference of political officers and civilians in the professional legislation of the army cannot be too severely rebuked and repressed. It is, and ever has been, the prolific cause of woeful calamities. It would, however, appear that the same mischievous spirit is at this critical juncture of our Indian history again at work to paralyse the freedom of action of the military commander in the field. When rebellion and military revolt are subdued, and the laws of the land can be safely administered, it will then be time enough for the civilian to appear on the scene and resume his own proper and legitimate functions. In such times as the present, what some writers term "simple mutiny" is *simply* nothing more or less than high treason, and, as such, punishable by death. The Gordian knot can only be cut by the sure and sharp agency of the sword, and, until *it is* cut, martial law must, for want of better, be the law of the land. But it behoves our military commanders to exercise this fearful power with a wise, and though stern, just discrimination. For—

> O, it is excellent
> To have a giant's strength, but it is tyrannous
> To use it like a giant."

The innocent should not be confounded with the guilty, and our brave European soldiers must be kept within bounds, and firmly prevented perpetrating wholesale butchery.

They cannot be allowed to soil their laurels in innocent blood.

Every subject who has raised an arm against the British Government in this desperately wicked revolt must, and even then inadequately, expiate his enormous guilt by *death*. All who have even passively revelled in these cruel devilries must suffer proportionately.

None of these can, with safety to the sacred cause of humanity, be ever again allowed to herd as human beings with those no longer their fellow men.

Society can know them no more. Vouchsafing the crowned miscreant of Delhi a fair trial before a *Council of War*, let him, on conviction of complicity, be summarily hung on the pinnacle of the Kootub Minar.

This would meet the wishes of those clamorous of appealing to the imagination of the natives, and prove a very suitable historical full stop to the cruel and blood-stained dynasty of Timour.

With this closing scene, might not the name of the accursed city be changed by proclamation, to

VICTORIAPORE?

And which, having thus fallen by assault, should be held to have become escheated. We might now purify, embellish, and ventilate it, on an improved European plan, re-people it with subjects untainted by the crimes of murder, and treason, and place the whole under the protection, and *surveillance* of fortified works.

To conceive it possible that the greater portion of the population of this city were not willingly identified with the revolted soldiery, is to betray the veriest ignorance of the native character of Hindustan. The inhabitants wildly conceived that our knell had sounded, and each rose, stone in hand, to aid and abet treason.

Had they been but loyally disposed, the unorganised and tumultuous Sepahees might have been expelled the city on their first display of open mutiny. But the citizens were *not* loyally disposed.

For this was not the revolt of slaves goaded into fiendish excesses by a hard, crushing system of tyranny, but the outbreak of ungrateful subjects, governed by the same laws which generations of Englishmen had *bled* and *fought* to obtain.

Have our immense body of military pensioners come forward at this crisis, to array themselves on the side of order and justice? At such a juncture, those who are not with us are against us, and must fare accordingly.

In all, and throughout this terrible mission of a stern, unfaltering retribution, let us wisely beware of viewing things through the bloody mist of passion and revenge.

And wherever it is possible, with safety to imperial interests, and the cause of civilization, we ought to exercise a magnanimous clemency. We cannot hold India, save with the Indians.

Appendix A.

MEMORANDUM ON THE AMALGAMATION OF SIKHS AND PUNJABEES WITH THE REGULAR ARMY, DRAWN UP, AND SUBMITTED FOR THE CONSIDERATION OF THE MOST NOBLE THE GOVERNOR-GENERAL OF INDIA.

LAHORE, *December* 12*th*, 1850.

1. The number of Sikhs and Punjabees to be entertained in the regular army should be strictly limited: probably, having all considerations in view, for the present, 200 per regiment would be a just proportion. Equivalent, with native commissioned, non-commissioned officers and drummers, to 17,168 Sikhs.

2. The Paol, or religious pledge of Sikh fraternity should on no account be interfered with—the Sikh should be permitted to wear his beard, and the hair of his head gathered up as enjoined by his religion. Any invasion, however slight, of these obligations would be construed into a desire to subvert his faith, would lead to evil consequences, and naturally inspire general distrust and alarm. Even those who have assumed the outward conventional characteristics of Sikhs, should not be permitted after entering the

British service to drop them. Their removing these distinctive peculiarities would be mischievously interpreted. If the recruit enters with the Kes, he must continue to wear the hair of the head in that fashion—as the odium of its removal, though even a voluntary act on his part would still attach to our system, and be viewed as an act of secession agreeable to us.

3. No men enlisted above 20 years of age; old Khalsa soldiers not admissible.

4. Muzbee Sikhs not eligible on any account, as their admission would destroy the whole tone and self-esteem of the regiment.

The low and inferior castes of Sikhs were not employed in the regular Sikh army, and had better be excluded in ours, *viz.*,—such as, 1. Barbers. 2. Ferrymen. 3. Fishermen. 4. Sweet meat sellers. 5. Bunneeahs. 6. Goldsmiths. 7. Gardeners. 8. Weavers. 9. Potters. 10. Washermen. 11. Bearers. 12. Tailors. 13. Dyers, 14. and Goojur Mahommedans.*

5. A Grunthee (priest) allowed to each regiment; ten rupees per mensem would be ample remuneration for the services of this individual, who should be a village or Deathee pastor, and not an Umritsir Doctor of Divinity. The latter description of person, might, and would probably prove dangerous in

* 1. Naic. 2. Mullah. 3. Cheerwar. 4. Hulwaie. 5. Khuttree. 6. Soonar. 7. Bhagwan. 8. Jullaha. 9. Koomar. 10. Dhobie. 11. Kuhar. 12. Dirzee. 13. Jullara. 14. Goojurs.

his ministry. The Grunth (Sikh Bible) should never be earried in military proeession, nor on any oeeasion ostentatiously displayed, for we require Sikhs and not Singhs in the ranks of the British native army.

6. Drunkenness and opium eating, are not so much Sikh vices, as vicious habits adopted by the old Khalsa soldiers, and contracted through the force of bad example, as is dram-drinking in the British army.

7. Levies should be drilled in distinct *Sikh* squads for the first three months, and by instructors selected for their equanimity and superior intelligence; abusive, *taunting* language, the cane, or violenee of any deseription strietly prevented on the part of instructors.

8. When perfected in their drill, *interspersed* throughout the regiment in equal proportion to each company. *Distinct Sikh* companies undesirable.

9. A proper allowanec of cooks and water-earriers to eaeh regiment should be coneeded. Three of eaeh description would enable the Sikh portion of a corps to eook and mess together when at regimental head quarters. Every means should be adopted to preserve their peculiar traits and social customs. For if they re-entered the pale of strict Hindooism, their value as a foreign military elass, and as sueh, useful counterpoise, would be altogether lost. Whilst firmly diseountenancing all *political* nationality, we might with great, and obvious advantage, uphold

the Sikhs in their comparative freedom from bigotted prejudices of caste, by affording them any reasonable aid and protection in defending their own distinctive characteristics of race, and by such a policy alone will this fusion of Sikhs into our regular native army prove to its fullest extent wise and advantageous.

10. Every artful ruse will be put into play by our Poorubeah Sepahees to disgust the Sikh recruit with our service; nor will sinister persuasion, or even intimidation, be wanting to browbeat him into abandoning the social peculiarities of his sect.

Should this succeed, the Sikh will sink into a mere low caste Hindoo. Shorn of his best attributes, and as a military exotic, lost to an army, particularly requiring new blood, his political worth as a new element would be destroyed.

11. The question offers itself, how far desirable it would be to form separate depôts for the enlistment and instruction of Sikhs and Punjabees, and after their drill was perfected, to send them in drafts, as required, to corps of the line? This arrangement would effectually protect their moral independence. and greatly assist the liberal views of Government as respecting their employment in the ranks of the British army.

12. It would be *very* necessary, indeed, that the commanding officers of native regiments of the line should be supplied with clear and specific instructions regarding their proper treatment, and furnished

with a list of the eligible castes from which to recruit, as also particularly desired to see that they meet with fair play. The Punjabee Mahommedan, from moral causes, rarely makes a good soldier. He is the Helot of the Punjab, and some years of our rule must elapse before, raised in his own self-esteem, he becomes a desirable class to recruit from.

J. S. HODGSON, BRIGADIER,
COMMANDING PUNJAB IRRE ULAR FORCE.

Appendix B.

(DEMI-OFFICIAL BOOK.)

DERA ISHMAEL KHAN,
28th March, 1852.

MY DEAR COURTENAY,

I have now concluded my annual inspection of the frontier, and have had every reason to be highly satisfied with what I saw.

I enclose for your perusal a letter received from Captain Jacob, commanding the 4th Punjab Cavalry The conduct of this detachment in thus charging, in cold blood, and in broad day, such a numerous body of well-armed Hill-men, (who had taken up a strong posetion), was truly heroic. The prudence of the attack under such circumstances I do not defend. But the men felt that they had the stigma of the Vidore outpost to wash out, and right boldly have they redeemed the character of their regiment. They charged right over a steep bank into the midst of the enemy, sword in hand, and under a fire of matchlocks. Unfortunately the carbines of this regiment have not yet arrived. I sincerely hope that his Lordship, the Governor-General, may be induced to favour my recommendation, that those who particularly distinguished themselves on this occasion may be rewarded with the Order of Merit. It is usual for native officers to offer their swords to be touched by their military superiors: this I declined doing when passing along Jacobs' posts, on account of the shameful misbehaviour of the Vidore outpost in surrendering without the slightest resistance.

All this, no doubt, determined the men on the first occasion, offering to make a full atonement for their recreant comrades' misconduct. Common justice, therefore, demands that I should use my best exertions to bring their gallant exploit forward for especial consideration, and I feel confident that it will not pass unrewarded.

There is but one opinion, that it was a most noble charge. And even the people of the country speak of it as an act that could only be performed by soldiers eating the salt of the Sirkar Company Bahadoor.

This inroad from the hills would never have taken place but for the co-operation given by the people of the plains—our own subjects.

I hear that some thirty have been apprehended who were engaged in this affair; all the particulars, I presume, will soon be laid before Government.

Do you ever read the "Lahore Chronicle?" as if so you must have been amused by one of Koap's editorials, wherein he sapiently observes that the Commander-in-Chief intends to summer at Umballa that he may be near the seat of war. The conduct of the 38th N. I. at the last hour sufficiently proves the correctness of my opinions, expressed in the little *brochure* I put forth, viz., that no man should be enlisted but on the clear understanding that he has enlisted for General Service to serve wherever he might be required. That most excellent order directing the embodiment of Sikhs and Punjabees into the regular army has, I fear, been very little acted up to by commanding officers of corps. A return showing the number of this class as yet enlisted into the several regiments of the line serving in the Punjab, would, I am inclined to believe, substantially prove the correctness of my doubts. Such a counterpoise is more than ever required. In a few years, if the present warlike spirit of the Sikh race is not fostered by admission into the ranks of the Native army, it will die out, and the Brahmin and Chuttree clique of Hindustan continue as heretofore to have it all their own way. The only way, in my opinion, to give *real effect* to the order of Government as regards the entertainment of these new subjects, will be by forming *Depôts* in the Punjaub, and sending drilled drafts to the several corps with their proportion of commissioned and non-commissioned native Officers, that thereby their proper professional status may be ensured them. Otherwise from not being fairly represented and protected in their grades by Officers of their own caste, both their efficiency, and zeal for the British service must be greatly diminished, and consequently the real object of Government in amalgamating them with our military subjects of Hindustan, palpably unattained. They will be merely an unhealthy excrescence, and not a wise and stringent counterpoise to the daily increasing cliqueism of our Sepahee army. The opportunity now lost will not be regained—for the Punjabees as a people are not a warlike race. The Sikhs lighted the fire of military enthusiasm, which, like all other fires, without being fed must gradually die out. I am really sorry to see such an opportunity lost. I sat down to write you a few lines, and I have inflicted upon you a lengthy epistle.

Always yours,

J. .S HODGSON.

To F. F. Courtenay, Esq.

Private Secretary to the Governor General.